Praise for Lewis Lapham
and *Gag Rule*

"Splendid . . . Lewis Lapham [is] in my opinion the most incisive essayist in America."　—Molly Ivins

"Not since Thomas Paine's *Common Sense* has there been such a clarion call to action. His argument is reasonable, clearly stated and refreshingly brief."　—*The Denver Post*

"Lewis Lapham eloquently, forcefully presents a painful history lesson—and a disturbing warning—in *Gag Rule* . . . Lapham brings the full force of his talents, utilizing both traditional and contemporary modes of rhetoric in [*Gag Rule*]. He dynamically builds a compelling moral argument capable of moving readers of all political persuasions to reflect deeply on the dangers facing our republic."　—*San Antonio Express-News*

"One of the strongest features of *Gag Rule* is Lewis Lapham's capacity to explain cogently the dynamic role of the mass media in the desensitized, disoriented condition on which the dominant economic and political systems depend. The unrelenting energy of Lapham's prose serves to expose the crude seductions that have replaced most sane political discourse with the murky PR mythology of unending infomercials."
　—*The Globe and Mail* (Toronto)

ABOUT THE AUTHOR

Lewis H. Lapham is the editor of *Harper's Magazine*, for which he writes an award-winning monthly column called "Notebook." He is the author of numerous books, including *Money and Class in America, 30 Satires,* and *Theater of War.* He has hosted two television series for PBS, *America's Century* and *Bookmark,* and his writing has appeared in *Vanity Fair,* the *National Review, Fortune, Forbes,* the *New York Times,* the *Observer* (London), and the the *Wall Street Journal,* among other publications. He lives in New York City.

LEWIS H. LAPHAM

GAG RULE

ON THE SUPPRESSION OF DISSENT
AND THE STIFLING OF DEMOCRACY

PENGUIN BOOKS

For my son, Andrew,

who enjoys an argument

PENGUIN BOOKS
Published by the Penguin Group
Penguin Group (USA) Inc., 375 Hudson Street, New York, New York 10014, U.S.A.
Penguin Group (Canada), 10 Alcorn Avenue, Toronto, Ontario, Canada M4V 3B2
   (a division of Pearson Penguin Canada Inc.)
Penguin Books Ltd, 80 Strand, London WC2R 0RL, England
Penguin Ireland, 25 St Stephen's Green, Dublin 2, Ireland (a division of Penguin Books Ltd)
Penguin Group (Australia), 250 Camberwell Road, Camberwell, Victoria 3124, Australia
   (a division of Pearson Australia Group Pty Ltd)
Penguin Books India Pvt Ltd, 11 Community Centre, Panchsheel Park,
   New Delhi–110 017, India
Penguin Group (NZ), cnr Airborne and Rosedale Roads, Albany,
   Auckland 1310, New Zealand (a division of Pearson New Zealand Ltd)
Penguin Books (South Africa) (Pty) Ltd, 24 Sturdee Avenue, Rosebank,
   Johannesburg 2196, South Africa

Penguin Books Ltd, Registered Offices: 80 Strand, London WC2R 0RL, England

First published in the United States of America by The Penguin Press,
a member of Penguin Group (USA) Inc. 2004
Published in Penguin Books 2005

10   9   8   7   6   5   4   3   2   1

Portions of this book appeared in different form in *Harper's Magazine*.

THE LIBRARY OF CONGRESS HAS CATALOGED THE HARDCOVER EDITION AS FOLLOWS:
Lapham, Lewis H.
Gag rule : on the suppression of dissent and the stifling of democracy /
Lewis H. Lapham.
p.   cm.
Includes bibliographical references and index.
ISBN 1-59420-017-3 (hc.)
ISBN 0 14 30.3502 9 (pbk.)
1. Freedom of speech—United States.   2. Mass media—Political aspects—United States.
3. Government, Resistance to—United States.   4. War on Terrorism, 2001–
5. Democracy—United States.   6. United States—Politics and government—2001–
I. Title.
JC599.U5L33   2004
323.44'3'0973—dc22   2004040044

Printed in the United States of America
Designed by Michelle McMillian

Contents

The spirit of liberty is the spirit
which is not too sure that it is right.

—JUDGE LEARNED HAND

Preface

When I was writing this book in the late autumn of 2003, dissent was a scarce commodity in the mainstream markets of American political opinion. Although the government in Washington was making no secret of either its incompetence or its dishonesty, the major retail outlets for the print and broadcast news were reluctant to decorate their holiday show windows with ugly questions about the botched liberation of Iraq or the paranoid devotion to a worldwide war on terror, about the rapidly diminishing store of the country's civil liberties or a faltering domestic economy propped up by heavy loans from foreign banks. The facts were hard to miss, but as had been their practice ever since President George W. Bush on September 12, 2001 enlisted America in the "Monumental Struggle Between Good and Evil," the providers of the country's best and brightest truths contrived to do so.

By the time the book was published in June 2004 it was possible to think that the news media had recovered their collective nerve and that the American democracy had regained its footing and its voice. As was to be expected in a presidential election year, the opposition candidate, in the person of Senator John F. Kerry, was loudly berating the incumbent administration for the failure of its policies both foreign and domestic; books fiercely critical of President George W. Bush's arrogance and duplicity led most of the nation's bestseller lists; on the television talk-show circuit numerous sources presumably well-informed (former government officials as well as journalists and historians) spoke to the derelictions of duty on the part of the intelligence agencies and the contempt for the Constitution in evidence at the Justice Department; Michael Moore's comic and seditious movie *Fahrenheit 9/11* was drawing record crowds to suburban shopping malls in Kentucky and Tennessee. Whether measured for its content or its sound levels, the volume of hostile commentary at odds with the wisdom in office in Washington seemed to hold out the promise of vigorous political argument over the course of the summer election campaign, possibly a meaningful debate about the character of the American democracy or the shape of its prospective future.

The hope was short-lived, the first signs of its futility showing up in July at the Democratic Party's nominating convention in Boston. Senator Kerry reported for duty with a brisk salute to the network television cameras; the delegates assembled in the Fleet Center received their hats and pom-poms with instructions to bite or hold their tongues. "Civility," the watchword, "values" preferred to "issues," no anger in the platitudes, the word, "liberal," deleted from the program. Making his way through the forest of photo opportunities in August and September, the candidate struck fetching poses with schoolchildren, apple trees, a surfboard, and a shotgun, but always he was careful to say nothing that might vex the governors of the New York Stock Exchange or offend the corporate sponsors who paid for the posters and the television time. With regard to the war in Iraq he expressed a view indistinguishable from the one favored by President Bush (a sorry mess, but "America's credibility is at stake," and failure therefore not an option); on the topics of health care, abortion, Social Security, gun control, gay marriage, and the minimum wage, he chose his words as delicately as if he were picking thorns from the stem of an American Beauty rose.

As the campaign drifted into the fog of vaguely-worded optimisms, the journalistic interest shifted to the long-ago war in Vietnam (how swift was Kerry's swift boat, for how many days and nights did Bush stand watch with the Texas National Guard), and the expressions of sharp-edged dissent were smothered under the pillows of patriotic cant. By early October the campaign had resolved itself into a single question—which of the two candidates looked more heroic in the costume of a military action figure capable of defending the American fatherland against its mortal enemies. President Bush proved to be a bigger hit in the role of Batman than did Senator Kerry in the role of Flash Gordon.

Nor had much been learned about the social, political, economic, and geophysical circumstances that confront the United States at the turn of the twenty-first century. Public opinion polls taken in March 2004 found that a majority of the American people blamed Saddam Hussein for the destruction of the World Trade towers, regarded global warming as a myth, and believed that the President of the United States didn't know how to tell a lie. The articles of faith remained securely in place seven months later on an Election Day that not only awarded President Bush a decisive plurality of the popular vote but also enlarged the Republican majorities in both the Senate and the House of Representatives. The London *Daily Mirror* published its tabulation of the result under the headline, *How can 59,054,087 people be so dumb?*, which was the same question that on the morning of November 3 confounded every late or early rising Democrat in Manhattan.

Among the company at lunch in a downtown restaurant catering to the media trades the conversation consisted of little else except the exchange of stunned silences. All present had been so certain that the election would go the other way. How could it not? The American people might be dumb, but were they also deaf and blind? Surely the facts spoke for themselves. Under a pretext demonstrably false, the Bush Administration had embarked the country on a disastrous and unnecessary war, darkened its economic future with a pall of toxic debt, assigned the care of its natural resources to the commercial interests certain to strip the land, poison the water, and pollute the air. What else did a voter need to know? Didn't people read the papers, look at the news broadcasts from Baghdad, listen to the voices of reason? Apparently not. What in New York had passed for the semblance of dissent had been seen by the national television audience as entertainment.

So unforeseen was the calamity at the polls that it was thought deserving of a higher order of politically scientific interpretation than ordinarily was to be found in a college civics class, and by noon on November 4 the *New York Times* had come up with no fewer than three op-ed page essays attributing the Democratic Defeat to the separation of the country's spiritual and intellectual powers. The historian Garry Wills explained that the eighteenth-century Enlightenment had come to grief in the Pentecostal wilderness south of Chattanooga, that "many more Americans believe in the Virgin Birth than in Darwin's theory of evolution." Maureen Dowd deplored the politics of fear and intolerance with which President George W. Bush had recruited "a devoted flock of evangelicals" to the banners of holy crusade; Thomas Friedman discovered himself in a country undreamed of in the philosophy Thomas Jefferson, where what has been lost is the distinction between church and state, where religion trumps science. The authors took no joy in their observations—possibly because their message was not much different from the propaganda delivered by Rush Limbaugh and the Reverend Jerry Falwell to the right-wing gospel crowd—but they testified to the existence of two Americas, one of them occupied by the virtuous souls in the great Midwestern heartland ("values voters," churchgoing

and culturally conservative), the other inhabited by cynical
apostates (nihilist at birth, often homosexual) trading foreign
currencies and languages in the secular cities on the nation's
seacoasts. Like it or not, the partition was encoded in the colors of the electoral map and therefore one to which we must
pay heed.

Writing for the same op-ed page on November 6,
Nicholas Kristof developed the evidence into a sermon. The
time had come, he said, for the Democratic Party to find its
way back to God. "I wish that winning were just a matter of
presentation," he said, "but it's not. It involves compromis-
ing on principles." For the wayward politicians among his
readers who might have lost their Bible in a Taiwanese bor-
dello or the belly of a whale, he suggested a few first steps on
the road to redemption—"Don't be afraid of religion"; argue theology with Republicans; "Hold your nose and work
with President Bush as much as you can because it's lethal to
be portrayed as obstructionist"; Democrats must learn to de-
fer to local sensibilities.

Senator Kerry swallowed the canard without a murmur, in
the manner of a well-bred Yale man accepting an oyster or a
grape; the national print and broadcast media produced
many fine words about the "healing" process binding up the
wounds of partisan bitterness and strife, and on November
16 the chastened and recently reduced minority of Democrats still present in the Senate deferred to the sensibility of
the nearest clergymen and named as their leader Harry Reid
of Nevada. Non-obstructionist and much admired for his
never having to hold his nose, Reid fit the description of a

Democrat saved by Jesus—a teetotaling Mormon, a former Capitol Hill police officer, opposed to abortion, co-sponsor of the constitutional amendment deeming it a crime to burn the flag, praised by his colleagues as "the kind of guy who'll make the trains run on time," as amiable as Mr. Rogers, "as strong as a new rope when he needs to be." Reid's rising to the office of Senate Minority Leader was symptomatic of the general distaste for the summer's brief experiment with the volatile substance of dissent. Instead of strengthening the freedoms of mind capable of preserving the American democracy, the presidential election campaign had reinforced the powers—of ignorance, fear, and superstition—that would destroy it.

ONE

An Audible Silence

The dissenter is every human being at those moments in his life when
he resigns momentarily from the herd and thinks for himself.
—ARCHIBALD MACLEISH

As a director of the U.S. government's ministry of propaganda during World War II, Archibald MacLeish knew that dissent seldom walks onstage to the sound of warm and welcoming applause. As a poet and later the librarian of Congress, he also knew that liberty has ambitious enemies, and that the survival of the American democracy depends less on the size of its armies than on the capacity of its individual citizens to rely, if only momentarily, on the strength of their own thought. We can't know what we're about, or whether we're telling ourselves too many lies, unless we can see or hear one another think out loud. Tyranny never has much trouble drumming up the smiles of prompt agreement, but a democracy stands in need of as many questions as its citizens can ask of their own stupidity and fear. Unpopular during even the happiest of stock market booms, in time of war dissent attracts the attention of the police. The parade marshals regard any wandering away from the line of march as unpatriotic and disloyal; unlicensed forms of speech come to be confused with treason and registered as crimes.

On the morning of September 11, 2001, the terrorist attacks on New York and Washington inflicted heavy losses on the frame of the American body politic; they also severely injured—not so obviously but no less surely—its animating principle and spirit. By nightfall the notion of a democratic republic founded on the premise of honest and sometimes sharply pointed speech had been placed in administrative detention, suspended until further notice, canceled because of rain; in the skyboxes of the national news media, august personages were reaffirming America's long-standing alliances with God, Moses, George Washington, and the hydrogen bomb. The barbarian was at the gates; civilization trembled in the balance, and now was not the time for any careless choice of word.* The next morning's newspapers called out the dogs of war.

---

*Together with the dead and wounded, there was an estimated $33.4 billion of structural damage, with all airline travel suspended, White House secretaries running for their lives, a frantic sealing off of the country's nuclear power stations as well as Mount Rushmore and Disneyland, the New York Stock Exchange out of commission and the city's mayoral primary election rescheduled, telephone communications down across large sectors of the Northeast, major-league baseball games canceled, the Capitol evacuated and most government offices in Washington closed until further notice, and the military services placed on high alert.

Robert Kagan in the *Washington Post*: "Congress, in fact, should immediately declare war. It does not have to name a country."

Steve Dunleavy in the *New York Post*: "The response to this unimaginable 21st century Pearl Harbor should be as simple as it is swift—kill the bastards. . . . Train assassins. . . . Hire mercenaries. . . . As for cities or countries that host these worms, bomb them into basketball courts."

Richard Brookhiser in the *New York Observer*: "The response to such a stroke cannot be legal or diplomatic—the international equivalent of mediation, or Judge Judy. This is what we have a military for. Let's not build any more atomic bombs until we use the ones we have."

Ann Coulter, in *National Review Online*: "We should invade their countries, kill their leaders, and convert them to Christianity."

On Friday, September 14, Congress equipped President George W. Bush with the power to "use all necessary and appropriate force against those nations, organizations, or persons he determines planned, authorized, committed, or aided the terrorist attacks." Passed unanimously by the Senate, the resolution in the House of Representatives met with only one dissenting vote, from Barbara J. Lee (D.-Calif.), who said that military action could not guarantee the safety of the country and that "as we act, let us not become the evil we deplore." A correct statement of the facts joined with a decent respect for the constitutional balancing of executive and legislative power, but not an opinion in tune with an orchestra playing "God Save the King." Within an hour Representative

Lee received several thousand e-mail death threats from patriots as far away as Guam. By Saturday, September 15, four days after the destruction of the World Trade Center, the nation's new set of red-white-and-blue ropelines had been placed around the perimeter of secure consensus. A choir of congressional voices gathered on the steps of the Capitol to sing "God Bless America"; President Bush stood suddenly revealed as a great leader, his stumbling and wooden speeches now blessed with the oratorical brilliance once ascribed to Winston Churchill and Abraham Lincoln; and during a series of resolute photo opportunities on various home fronts (with Billy Graham at the National Cathedral in Washington, among firemen and rescue workers in New York, with his senior advisers at Camp David), he gradually escalated the rhetorical terms of engagement from the "First War of the Twenty-first Century" to the "Monumental Struggle of Good Versus Evil."

Alive to the magnitude of the task at hand, the government busied itself over the next six weeks with the fortification of its own safety and authority, alerting the public to the chance of an attack on Disneyland or the Golden Gate Bridge, restricting the freedoms of civilian movement and expression, hiding Vice President Dick Cheney in an underground bunker in suburban Maryland, bringing up to combat strength the national reserves of xenophobic paranoia. The Pentagon issued a much-strengthened National Security Strategy, replacing the cold war theories of deterrence and containment with the strategies of "preemptive strike" and "anticipatory self-defense." On September 18 the Justice

Department published an interim regulation allowing non-citizens suspected of terrorism to be detained without charge for forty-eight hours or "an additional reasonable period of time" in the event of an "emergency or other extraordinary circumstance." Asked on September 26 for comment on a possibly seditious opinion overheard on network television, Ari Fleischer, the White House press secretary, informed the correspondents at his daily press briefing, "There are reminders to all Americans that they need to watch what they say, watch what they do."*

The members of Congress didn't need reminders. During the months of October and November every White House request for money or silence was met with an obedient show of hands. No points of order or objection, no memorable speech, nothing but the steady murmur of approval and the quiet hum of praise. On October 2 the Senate voted, unanimously and without debate, to fund a $60 billion missile defense system that to the best of nearly everybody's knowledge couldn't hit its celestial targets and offered no defense against the deadly weapons (smallpox virus, dynamite stuffed into a barrel of nuclear waste) likely to be hand-delivered by terrorists driving rented speedboats or stolen

---

*Fleischer was responding to a remark made by Bill Maher, the host of ABC's *Politically Incorrect*. Maher had said that the nineteen Arab terrorists aboard the hijacked airliners on the morning of September 11 were not cowards but that it was cowardly for the United States to launch cruise missiles on targets thousands of miles away. The show's sponsors FedEx and Sears withdrew their advertising, and ABC canceled it.

trucks. Senator Carl Levin (D.-Mich.), chairman of the Armed Services Committee, explained the absence of discussion by saying that in times of trouble "we have no need to create dissent while we need unity." Three weeks later on the other side of Capitol Hill, the House of Representatives passed an "economic stimulus package" that administered the bulk of the $101 billion stimulus to the wealthiest of the country's business interests. Asked about the apparent senselessness of the repeal of the corporate alternative minimum tax, Dick Armey (R.-Tex.), the House majority leader, justified the gifts ($1.4 billion to IBM, $833 million to GM, $671 million to GE, and so on) by saying, "This country is in the middle of a war. Now is not the time to provoke spending confrontations with our Commander-in-Chief."*

Similar flows of sentiment stifled the asking of awkward questions when, on October 26, President Bush signed the USA PATRIOT Act, 342 pages of small print that few members of Congress took the trouble to read, but that nevertheless permitted Attorney General John Ashcroft to expand telephone and Internet surveillance, extend the reach of wiretaps, obtain warrants to review the borrowings from public libraries, and open financial and medical records to

---

*In answer to questions as to why the $15 billion soothing of economic wounds suffered by the airline industry didn't include any money, none whatsoever, for the 150,000 airline workers who had lost their jobs in September, Armey observed that any help extended to such people "is not commensurate with the American spirit."

searches for suspicious behavior and criminal intent.* Like the missile appropriations, the USA PATRIOT Act passed into law without a public hearing or debate, its character described by Representative Barney Frank (D.-Mass.) as "a bill drafted by a handful of people in secret, subject to no committee process . . . immune from amendment."† In the event that all present might not be familiar with the new and revised edition of the Constitution, Attorney General Ashcroft appeared before the Senate Judiciary Committee on December 6 to say, "To those who scare peace-loving people with phantoms of lost liberty, my message is this: your tactics only aid terrorists, for they erode our national unity and diminish our resolve. They give ammunition to America's enemies and pause to America's friends."

America's friends weren't slow to take their cues. During the first week of the country's abruptly revoked special arrangement with Providence (the land of the free and the home of the brave no longer preserved from harm by the virtue of its inhabitants and the grace of its geography), hundreds of thousands of American flags appeared in store

---

*Two weeks later the president signed an emergency order allowing him to remand to a military tribunal any foreign national about whom he had "reason to believe" a rumor of cohabitation with a terrorist organization, a nihilist author, or an anarchist idea. He conceded the point that the order set aside "the principles of law and the rules of evidence."

†The bill passed by the Senate by a vote of 98 to 1, Russell Feingold (D.-Wis.) voicing the only dissent. "The new law," he said, "goes into a lot of areas that have nothing to do with terrorism and a lot to do with the government and the FBI having a list of things they want to do."

windows, at bridge crossings, on the fenders of city limousines and country pickup trucks; "out of respect to visitors' sensibilities," officials at the Baltimore Museum of Art removed from exhibition a painting entitled *Terrorist;* by a vote of 200 to 1 the Pennsylvania House of Representatives passed a bill requiring the state's public schools to begin every day's classes with a recitation of the Pledge of Allegiance or the singing of the national anthem; in the midst of delivering a commencement address in Sacramento, California, one of that city's prominent newspaper publishers was forced off the stage for saying that the events of September 11 might call upon the American people to decide which of their civil liberties they were willing to give up "in the name of security"; in Washington, D.C., the American Council of Trustees and Alumni (ACTA) published a guide to the preferred forms of free speech under the title *Defending Civilization,* the authors of the pamphlet being careful to make their curtsy to "the robust exchange of ideas" so "essential to a free society," before going on to say that the nation's universities—*all* the nation's universities—had failed to respond to the provocations of September 11 with a proper degree of "anger, patriotism and support of military intervention."* As evidence for its assertions the guide offered a list of 115 subversive remarks

---

*Among the prominent conservative and neoconservative ideologues identified as ACTA's leading lights the pamphlet lists Lynne V. Cheney, the vice president's wife and a fellow at the American Enterprise Institute; Martin Peretz, editor in chief of *The New Republic;* Irving Kristol, coeditor of *The Public Interest;* and William Bennett, editor of *The Book of Virtues.*

culled from college newspapers, or overheard on university campuses by the council's vigilant informants during the fifty-one days between September 14 and November 4.*

Nor did the doorkeepers of the national news and entertainment media need to be reminded that dissent was bad for business as well as un-American and wrong. The romance of war boosts ratings and sells advertisements, and once caught up in the glories of a tale told by Tom Clancy or Rudyard Kipling, the editors of responsible newspapers remove contraband opinion from the typescripts of known polemicists, and the producers of network talk shows decorate the studio chairs with generals who can read the maps. On the bright new morning of America's war against "all the world's evildoers," one that Secretary of Defense Donald Rumsfeld guessed might last as long as forty years, Dan Rather enlisted for the duration, proud to inform the viewers of the *CBS Evening News* that "George Bush is the president. Wherever he wants me to line up, just tell me where." *Vanity Fair* quarantined the tone of irony, as did the publishers of *Time, Newsweek,* and the *Wall Street Journal.* Ted Koppel introduced his *Nightline* audience to Arundhati Roy, an Indian novelist critical of American foreign policy, with a word of caution: "Some

---

*Among the prominent sentiments deemed treasonous: "We have to learn to use courage for peace instead of war" (professor of religious studies, Pomona College); "[I]ntolerance breeds hate, hate breeds violence and violence breeds death, destruction and heartache" (student, University of Oklahoma); "[We should] build bridges and relationships, not simply bombs and walls" (speaker at Harvard Law School); "Our grief is not a cry for war" (poster at New York University).

of you, many of you, are not going to like what you hear tonight. You don't have to listen. But if you do, you should know that dissent sometimes comes in strange packages."

Similarly worried about possible misinterpretation and alarmed by reports of a pacifist protest assembling some-where in the streets of Georgetown, Peter Beinart, editor at *The New Republic,* advised the magazine's readers to beware the sins of ambiguity and doubt. "The nation," he said, "is now at war. And in such an environment, domestic political dissent is immoral without a prior statement of national sol-idarity, a choosing of sides." Erik Sorenson, president of MSNBC, explained the absence of on-camera talking heads opposed to the policies of the Bush administration by saying that he couldn't find any credible experts willing to make patently stupid or seditious arguments; to a reporter from the *New York Times* he said that apart from the ravings of a few Hollywood celebrities, there wasn't enough dissent in the country "to warrant coverage." The regiment of right-wing radio talk-show hosts under the command of captain Rush Limbaugh meanwhile pressed home its attacks on the writings of Susan Sontag and Noam Chomsky, and when it came time in late October to send the army to Afghanistan, the Pentagon's heavily censored film footage was gratefully received by news executives eager to bring urgent bulletins, every hour on the hour, from the frontiers of dread. If the dispatches from the few reporters actually on the ground in Kabul or Mazar-i-Sharif tended to present the Taliban as ragged fugitives—lightly armed, often barefoot, their cause lost without a fight—the editors in Washington and New

York reinforced the adjectives, airbrushed out the footage of dogs devouring dead bodies on the road to Kunduz, dressed up the headlines with "monsters" and "diabolical henchmen" overseeing "a web of hate."*

President Bush had informed the members of the United Nations on November 10 that civilization's War Against Barbarism didn't afford the luxury of diplomatic hesitation ("either you are with us, or you are with the terrorists"), and by the end of November the big-time news and entertainment media were papering the broadcast booths with swaths of geopolitical commentary that went well with the waving of flags. The viewing audience wasn't expected to know what the words meant; it was supposed to listen to them in the way that schoolchildren listen to a military band playing "Stars and Stripes Forever" on the Washington Mall, or to Ray Charles singing "God Bless America" in Yankee Stadium.†

---

*Geraldo Rivera went off to the Khyber Pass with a pistol in his luggage, informing his viewers on Fox News that he would consider killing Osama bin Laden if the chance presented itself somewhere on the snowy heights of Tora Bora.

†Thucydides in his *History of the Peloponnesian War* remarks on the way in which loud and mindless shouting of patriotic slogans silenced the expression of dissent in Athens prior to that city's invasion of Sicily in 415 B.C. The Athenian assembly was so fond of its enthusiasm for war that no citizen dared speak against the policies of forward deterrence, preemptive strike, anticipatory self-defense. "To think of the future and wait," says Thucydides, "was merely another way of saying one was a coward; any idea of moderation was just another attempt to disguise one's unmanly character; ability to understand the question from all sides meant that one was totally unfitted for action; fanatical enthusiasm was the mark of a real man . . . anyone who held violent opinions could always be trusted, and anyone who objected to them became a suspect" (translation by Rex

If by Christmas Day the voices of dissent couldn't make it past the security guards at the White House or CNN, they could be heard plainly in the distance beyond the ropelines of consensus—in literary journals of modest circulation, in the letters to the editors of the *Washington Post* or the *New York Times,* among a scattering of guests on National Public Radio, in the farther reaches of C-SPAN and the Internet. Sufficiently numerous to suggest the presence of a formidable minority, they were loud enough to raise the possibility of a genuine political argument about the character of the American commonwealth, well enough grounded in the lessons of American history to know that dissent is not a synonym for anarchy. Most simply understood, dissent consists of nothing else except the right to say no, to volunteer a second or third opinion; defined as another word for liberty, it is the freedom to conceive of the future as an empty canvas or a blank page, no further away than the next sentence, the next best guess, the next sketch for the painting of a life portrait that might or might not become a masterpiece.

Although not obliged to sign petitions or march in protests, dissent recruited to a public cause expresses its allegiance to country as the search for a better question and a

---

Warner). Athens mustered an invasion fleet conforming to the current Pentagon doctrine of "overwhelming force" (134 triremes, expensively gilded; impressive numbers of archers, slingers, and javelin throwers; merchant vessels stocked with soothsayers and cavalry horses), and on a sunny day in July 415 B.C., trumpets blew, priests poured wine into golden bowls, and "by far the most costly and splendid" expedition "ever sent out by a single city" sailed for Sicily and its appointment with destruction.

straighter answer, what Archibald MacLeish understood to be the difference between a safe yes and an unwelcome no, and what Teddy Roosevelt had in mind in 1918 when he disagreed with President Woodrow Wilson's theory of World War I: "To announce that there must be no criticism of the president or that we are to stand by the president right or wrong, is not only unpatriotic and servile, but it is morally treasonable to the American public." Henry Steele Commager, the Columbia University historian and one of the very few American authors willing to exercise his First Amendment right to free speech during the McCarthy era, believed that a democracy worthy of the name depends for its existence upon the capacity of its citizens for what he called "moral agitation." Vilified in the jingo press as a "Communist" and "a termite undermining the Constitution," Commager in 1947 published in *Harper's Magazine* an essay, "Who Is Loyal to America?," that still deserves an attentive reading:

It is easier to say what loyalty is not than what it is. It is not conformity. It is not passive acquiescence to the status quo. It is not preference for everything American over everything foreign. It is not an ostrich-like ignorance of the other countries and other institutions. It is not the indulgence in ceremony—a flag salute, an oath of allegiance, a fervid verbal declaration. It is not a particular creed, a particular vision of history, a particular body of economic practices, a particular philosophy.

It is a tradition, an ideal, and a principle. It is a willingness to subordinate every private advantage for the larger good. It is an appreciation of the rich and diverse contributions that can come from the most varied sources. It is allegiance to the traditions that have guided our greatest statesmen and inspired our most eloquent poets—the traditions of freedom, equality, democracy, tolerance, and the tradition of Higher Law, of experimentation, cooperation, and pluralism. It is the realization that America was born of revolt, flourished on dissent, became great through experimentation.

The country was founded by dissenters. The Protestant signatories to the Mayflower Compact (that is, protesters) arrived in Massachusetts Bay with little else except a cargo of contraband words. Possessed of what they believed to be truthful refutations of the lies told by God's enemies in Rome and London, they settled the New England wilderness as an act of intellectual opposition framed on the premise of what they called "the quarrel with Providence." Within the provinces of the religious spirit over the course of the last four centuries, the further flourishing of dissent gave rise to the amendment of the Protestant faith to fit the answers preferred by Quakers, Baptists, Mennonites, Mormons, Christian Scientists, and Jehovah's Witnesses, to the abolitionist and civil rights movements, to the cause of women's rights and the conscientious objections to every war in American history.

Transferred in the eighteenth century to the precincts of secular argument, the quarrel with Providence resulted in Thomas Paine's *Common Sense,* the founding document of the American Revolution. First printed in January 1776, the pamphlet persuaded readers everywhere in the colonies to exchange a grievance for a cause and so transfer the gestures of incoherent protest into the settled purpose of rebellion. Paine proceeded from the seditious statement that "as in absolute governments the King is law, so in free countries, the law ought to be King," forcing the point of his argument well beyond the limits of objection voiced by the propertied malcontents in Connecticut and Virginia who had been complaining of the trade restrictions imposed by a distant and unrepresentative Parliament. Not enough, said Paine, merely to reach the accommodation of an "ordered liberty" with the agents of the English Crown. Better to separate completely from "the natural disease of monarchy," a grotesque and unjust "form of government, which so impiously invades the prerogative of heaven." It was, said Paine, "the birthday of a new world," and the time was at hand to do away with hereditary successions, class privilege, entitled aristocracy. His pamphlet ran to an edition of 150,000 copies, and the bestselling signs of a national resolve encouraged Thomas Jefferson to borrow Paine's reasoning when he came to the writing, six months later in Philadelphia, of the Declaration of Independence.

The abundance of Paine's writing flows from the spring of his optimism, and during the twenty years of his engagement in both the American and the French Revolutions, he counted himself a "friend of the world's happiness." No matter what question he takes up (the predicament of women, the practice of slavery, or the organization of governments), he approaches it with generous impulse and benevolent purpose. Opposed

to all things "monarchical or aristocratical," invariably in favor of a new beginning and a better deal, Paine speaks to his
hope for the rescue of mankind in a voice that hasn't been
heard in American politics for the last thirty years.

> When it shall be said in any country in the world, my poor
> are happy; neither ignorance nor distress is to be found
> among them; my jails are empty of prisoners, my streets
> of beggars; the aged are not in want; the taxes are not op-
> pressive . . . when these things can be said, then may that
> country boast its constitution and its government.

> I do not believe in the creed professed by the Jewish
> church, by the Roman church, by the Greek church, by the
> Turkish church, by the Protestant church, or by any church
> that I know of. My own mind is my own church.

By comparison with the machine-made cant pushed forth
by the government now in Washington, the old words bring
with them the sound of water in a desert, and in December
2001, when I found myself rereading Paine's *Age of Reason*
and *Rights of Man* (as an antidote to what was being said by
Donald Rumsfeld and his fuglemen in both the parlor and
the tabloid press), I thought that the well-publicized search
for the meaning in the ashes of the World Trade Center con-
ceivably might lead to candid debate about the future course
of what Benjamin Franklin had recognized as the American
political experiment. Why not? It wasn't as if large numbers
of people didn't understand that by declaring "war on ter-

rorism" the Bush administration had declared war on an unknown enemy and an abstract noun, that we might as well be sending the 101st Airborne Division to conquer lust, annihilate greed, imprison the sin of pride. Although Osama bin Laden was still nowhere to be found, the Taliban were gone from Afghanistan, no further terrorist attacks had come against any American target, and on the editorial pages of the national newspapers at least some of the contributors had begun to appreciate the damage done to the economic and political theory that over the last twenty years had achieved the standing of holy writ. Erected by the household sophists in the Reagan administration and strengthened by their successors in the Bush and Clinton administrations, the intellectual foundation for the country's wealth and happiness rested on four pillars of imperishable wisdom:

1. Global capitalism is the eighth wonder of the world, a light unto the nations, and the answer to everybody's prayers. Nothing must interfere with its sacred mysteries and omniscient judgment.

2. Big government is by inclination Marxist, by definition wasteful and incompetent, a conspiracy of fools indifferent to the welfare of the common man. The best government is no government.

3. The art of politics (embarrassingly human and therefore corrupt) is subordinate to the science of economics (reassuringly abstract and therefore perfect). What need of political principle or philosophy when it is the money markets that set policy, pay the troops, distrib-

ute alms? What need of statesmen, much less politicians, when it isn't really necessary to know their names or remember what they say?

4. History is at an end. The new world economic order vanquished the last of the skeptics by refuting the fallacy of Soviet communism. Having reached the final stopping place on the road to ideological perfection, mankind no longer need trouble itself with any new political ideas.

All four pillars of imperishable wisdom perished on the morning of September 11, reduced within an hour to the incoherence of the rubble in Liberty Street. By noon even the truest of true believers knew that they had been telling themselves a fairy tale. If not to big government, then where else did the friends of laissez-faire economics look for the rescue of their finances and the saving of their lives? If not the agencies of big government, who then brought the ambulances from as far away as Albany or sent the firemen into the doomed buildings with no promise of a finder's fee? It wasn't the free market that hijacked the airplanes and cross-promoted them into bombs, or Adam Smith's invisible hand that cut the throats of the pilots on what they thought was a flight to Los Angeles. History apparently was still a work in progress.

Together with the headlines blowing the bugles of imperial advance, the newspapers during the autumn of 2001 had been reporting daily proofs of courage and intelligence on the part of a citizenry formerly presumed decadent or deceased—not only a show of flags but also people everywhere in the country giving their money and effort to whatever need was near at hand—unpaid rescue workers clearing the wreckage in Lower Manhattan; $850 million in emergency funds contributed by individuals as well as corporations; generous upwellings of tolerance and compassion among people of different ages, races, colors, and sexual orientations, their regard for one another grounded in the recognition that the modifying adjectives—"black," "gay," "white," "native," "Asian," "Hispanic"—mattered less than the noun—"American."

I didn't think it impossible that something of the same public-spiritedness might find a voice in Congress, or that the list of questions gathering on the Internet—about the purpose of the country's foreign policy and the distributions of its domestic wealth—might somehow come to the attention of Tom Brokaw or Peter Jennings and so present an opportunity to ask what we mean by such phrases as "public service," "civic interest," and the "common good." Informed argument about why and how America had come to be perceived as a dissolute empire; instructive doubts cast on the supposed omniscience of the global capital markets; a distinction drawn between the ambitions of the American national security state and the collective well-being of the American citizenry. I could imagine the argument falling along the division between people who would continue Ben Franklin's experiment and those who think the experiment has gone far enough, and if I couldn't frame all the questions that might well be asked, I could think of at least a few:

How high a price do we set on the head of freedom? If we delete another few paragraphs from the Bill of Rights (for our own protection, of course, in the interests of peace, prosperity, and carefree summer vacations), what do we ask of the government in return for our silence in court? Do we wish to remain citizens of a republic, or do we prefer some form of autocracy in which a genial man on horseback assures us that repression is good for the soul? With what secular faith do we match the zeal of militant Islam and combat the enmity of the impoverished peoples of the earth to whom the choice between war and peace presents itself as a choice of no significance? How define the American democracy as a *res publica* for which we might willingly give up our lives—our own lives, not the lives of hired mercenaries? And of what, if anything, does the *res publica* consist?

The questions remain unasked, the occasion for debate indefinitely postponed. If on New Year's Day 2002 I had hoped that the attacks on New York and Washington might give us pause for thought, by the first week in February I understood that we lack a national forum in which to hear the questions and that language degraded into propaganda doesn't lend itself to sustained argument or inspired eloquence. In his State of the Union address to Congress on January 29, President Bush pronounced the sentence of doom on Saddam Hussein ("America will do what is necessary to ensure our nation's security. . . . I will not wait on events, while dangers gather"); five days later in New Orleans, the choreographers of the game and pregame entertainment at the Super Bowl set the words to music. Billed as "A Celebration of America" the six-hour hymn to victory deployed theme music from the soundtrack of *Star Wars,* film footage of America the Beautiful (Mount Rushmore, the White House, amber waves of grain), four ex-presidents reading from the speeches and letters of Abraham Lincoln, Paul McCartney playing the guitar and Mariah Carey singing "The Star-Spangled Banner," a reenactment of the raising of the flag on Iwo Jima, festive greetings from a Marine unit in far-off Afghanistan ("the most heavily armed Super Bowl party in the world"), a Budweiser beer commercial in which the brewer's trademark Clydesdale horses bring their wagon to New York and kneel in homage to the diminished skyline. The halftime show brought with it Bono and his band on a heart-shaped stage, singing "Where the Streets Have No Name" against the backdrop of a diaphanous scrim bearing the names of all those who had perished in the inferno of the World Trade Center—the names of firemen, airline passengers, policemen, office workers, all rising, like the credits on a movie screen, into the strobe-lit heavens of the Superdome.*

For the next thirteen months the hope of a national political awakening was smothered under the pillows of cant. For having had the temerity to question the premise of Washing-

---

*The stadium perimeter was defended by two thousand men in uniform; the seventy-eight thousand fans were thoroughly searched before being herded into their seats two hours prior to kickoff to provide captive applause for the songs of liberty.

ton's war on terror, the actor Tim Robbins was removed from the list of guests invited to a summer festival at the Baseball Hall of Fame in Cooperstown, New York; Chris Hedges, a *New York Times* reporter, began a commencement address at Rockford College in Illinois with the truism "War in the end is always about betrayal; betrayal of the young by the old, soldiers by politicians, and idealists by cynics," and within a matter of minutes his microphone was unplugged and his presence booed off the stage; in Portland, Oregon, a state senator proposed a bill identifying as a terrorist any person taking part in a street demonstration intended to disrupt traffic, conviction of the crime bringing with it an automatic sentence of twenty-five years to life in prison.

President Bush meanwhile mounted flag-draped rostra at West Point and Virginia Military Institute to proclaim America "the single surviving model of human progress" and to threaten with the wrath of eagles "men of mad ambition"; in Texas and Maine he hopped out of golf carts to tell the traveling White House press corps that "regime change" was coming soon to downtown Baghdad.* Senior administration officials found time in their busy schedules to inform the American television audience that other terrorist attacks were both imminent and inevitable. Vice President Dick Cheney on May 19: "The prospects of a future attack against the United States are almost certain . . . not a matter of if, but

---

*Prior to teeing off on the fifth hole at Kennebunkport, the president said, "I call upon all nations to do everything they can to stop these terrorist killers. Thank you. Now watch this drive."

when." Robert Mueller III, the director of the FBI, on May 20:
"There will be another terrorist attack. We will not be able to
stop it." Donald Rumsfeld, secretary of defense, on May 21:
"It's only a matter of time." The Defense Department meanwhile bolstered the president's credibility with distributions
of documents, supposedly top-secret, that sketched out the
Pentagon's tactical solutions to the problem of blitzkrieg—
the advantages of a simultaneous attack from three directions balanced against the surprise of a swift commando
raid; requisitions for three hundred thousand troops compared with those for only eighty thousand; something grandil-
oquent and imperial along the lines of the Japanese assault
on Pearl Harbor as opposed to something stylish and postmodern with parachutes, two divisions of light infantry, and
a diffusion of Turkish auxiliaries.

Against every precedent of international law, in violation
of the United Nations Charter, and without consent of the
American Congress, the Bush administration was preparing
to sack a heathen city that had done it no demonstrable
harm, but the news media were content to forgo any moral
or legal questions in favor of their obsession with the logis-
tics. Competing television networks scheduled different time
slots for the forthcoming fireworks display—before and after November's congressional election; in early January when
the weather around Baghdad improved; in April 2003 because the air force needed six months to replenish the inventory of precision-guided bombs consumed by the retail
markets in Afghanistan. Competing newspaper columnists
advanced competing adjectives to characterize the "extreme

danger" presented to "the entire civilized world," but none of them offered evidence proving that Saddam possessed weapons likely to harm anybody who didn't happen to be living in Iraq; important military authorities appeared on the Sunday morning talk shows to endorse policies of forward deterrence and anticipatory self-defense ("America will act against emerging threats before they are fully formed"), but none of them could think of a good reason why Saddam would make the mistake of attacking the United States. On July 22, Defense Secretary Rumsfeld issued a secret directive to special operations forces, allowing them to "capture terrorists for interrogation or, if necessary, to kill them" anywhere in the world; two weeks later, in its lead editorial for August 3, *The Economist* summed up in two sentences the consensus of approved opinion: "The honest choices now are to give up and give in, or to remove Mr. Hussein before he gets his bomb. Painful as it is, our vote is for war." Give up to whom? Give in to what? The questions were neither asked nor answered. The government didn't stoop to simpleminded explanations, and the emissaries from the print and broadcast media were content to accept the purpose of a policy apparently directed at nothing else than the fear of the future, that always dark and dangerous place where, in five years or maybe ten, something bad is bound to happen.

On the following day, August 4, Senator Joseph Biden (D.-Del.), chairman of the Foreign Relations Committee, granted an audience to the television cameras on Capitol Hill in which he said, "I believe there probably will be a war with Iraq. The only question is, is it alone, is it with others, and how long and how costly will it be?"

During the last weeks of August the newspapers brought daily reports of the American armada gathering in the Middle East (a fleet of merchant ships already at sea heavily burdened with armored vehicles, helicopters, and large stores of ammunition), and the rumors of imminent invasion served as prologue to the Republican victories in the November congressional elections. When Tom Daschle (D.-S.Dak.), the Senate minority leader, suggested that the Bush administration's rush to foreign war might be seen as a function of its domestic political ambitions, Trent Lott (R.-Miss.), the Senate majority leader, smeared him with the mud of treason: "Who is the enemy here? The president of the United States or Saddam Hussein?"*

---

*The majority leader borrowed from the cynicism of Reichsmarschall Hermann Göring, who diagrammed for the judges at Nuremberg the simplicities of successful propaganda: "All you have to do is tell them that they're being attacked, denounce the pacifists for lack of patriotism and exposing the country to danger. It works the same in any country."

On the same day that Lott questioned Daschle's patriotism, Secretary Rumsfeld asked the FBI to investigate the appearance in the *New York Times* of classified planning options for the invasion of Iraq, suggesting that whoever leaked the information should be sent to prison. Two weeks later Tom DeLay (R.-Tex.), majority leader of the House of Representatives, slandered any and all Democrats objecting to the Bush administration's war policy. "They don't want to protect the American people," DeLay said. "They will do anything, spend all the time and resources they can, to avoid confronting evil."

The Justice Department and the FBI supported the election campaign with upgrades of the USA PATRIOT Act (more stringent guidelines governing "the use of confidential informants") and with the steady hoisting of signal flags (yellow, orange, red) announcing the approach of doom. Ten murders committed in early October by two American assassins at large in the Washington suburbs lent further credence to the government's story of never-ending threat, and by election day the American people apparently had become so heavily sedated with the drug of fear that the opinion polls were showing a 70 percent approval rating for President Bush, 60 percent in favor of sending the army to exterminate Saddam, four of every five respondents saying that they gladly would give up as many of their civil rights and liberties as might be needed to pay the ransom for their illusory safety.

Which might have been all well and good and a blessing for America's newfound theory of immortal empire if the numbers could be believed. The anecdotal evidence was by no means so straightforward as the arithmetic. My own observations traveling around the country during the months of September and October suggested the widespread presence of attitudes more heavily weighted with ambiguity and doubt. In California, Texas, Oregon, and Iowa, I could find little trace or sign of the militant spirit presumably eager to pat the dog of war. The responses to the president's repeated attempts to explain the reasons for a descent on Baghdad (America "did not ask for this present challenge, but we accept it") often bordered on sarcasm:

"Who does the man think he's talking to—to people so stupid that they can't see through the window of his lies?"

"Who can take seriously the reasoning of a man armed with so few facts?"

"Why must the security of every other nation in the world be subordinated to the comfort of the United States?"

"I thought we learned from our mistake in Vietnam that we don't know how to do regime change."

Neither the candor nor the intelligence of the questions being asked beyond the perimeter of Washington reached the floor of Congress on October 11, 2002, during its brief discussion of the "Authorization for the Use of Military Force in Iraq." Instead of arguing with one another, the politicians read prepared statements into the C-SPAN cameras, striking handsome poses, producing certificates of their moral character and worth, expressing their "deep concern" for human suffering and their "profound awareness" of the distinction between war and peace. The time taken up quibbling over the syntax and punctuation of the authorization rescued all present from the embarrassment of having to talk about the abdication of their legislative authority, and after the pretense of a debate that lasted less than a week, the joint resolution investing President George W. Bush with the power to order an American invasion of Iraq whenever it occurred to him to do so, for whatever reason he might deem glorious or convenient, was hurried into law by docile majorities in both a Senate (77 to 23) and a House of Representatives (296 to 133) much relieved to escape the chore—tiresome, unpopular, time-consuming, poorly paid—of republican self-government.*

A chorus of senior editorial voices followed the scripts prepositioned by the White House and the Pentagon, solemnly interpreting the policy of preemptive bombing, precision guided and mercifully brief, as a form of compassionate conservatism. It wasn't that America would go willingly to war, but neither could it allow the forces of evil to recruit a quorum in the deserts of Mesopotamia. War was never easy and not to be undertaken lightly, but catastrophe loomed on both the far and near horizons, and who could doubt that Saddam must be destroyed? Not Citigroup or ExxonMobil; not the *New York Times,* CBS, the *Washington Post,* NBC, the *Wall Street Journal,* Fox News, or *USA Today.*

Prior to the autumn congressional elections, the Democratic candidates uttered barely a squeak of objection to the administration's war policy, and on November 7 the Republican Party added the capture of the Senate to its possession of the White House, the Supreme Court, and the House of Representatives, thus shifting the de facto imbalance of

---

*A few forthright speeches proved exceptions to the rule of cowardice. In the House of Representatives, Nancy Pelosi (D.-Calif.) counted the costs to the American economy of an unnecessary war waged to pay the bill for the administration's incompetent diplomacy. In the Senate, Robert Byrd (D.-W.Va.) declaimed against both the ignoble scurrying to kiss the feet of power ("Haste is blind and improvident, Mr. President, blind and improvident") and the betrayal of the Constitution ("What a shame. Fie upon us, the Congress! Fie upon us!") He addressed his remarks to an all but empty chamber, only three senators extending him the courtesy of an audience.

power further to the evangelical right. On November 8, the day after the votes were counted, the United States presented the United Nations with Resolution 1441, delivering to Saddam Hussein the ultimatum of war unless he complied, within forty-five days, to the Security Council's demand for "unconditional and unrestricted access to all of Iraq."

For the next three months the authorities in charge of what passed for the national political argument talked of little else except the long-postponed and soon-arriving duel in the sun: Would Saddam bow to the American fiat? Could the United Nations weapons inspectors find a nuclear warhead hidden in a palm tree or a palace? Why were the Germans and the French so reluctant to see the light of reason or accept the verdict of history? Was America an empire, and, if so, who had given empires a bad name; where and how had they come to be known for their corruption instead of their glory? Senior figures in the Bush administration carried their military sales promotion into all the major markets—the president to Capitol Hill with the State of the Union address, Secretary of Defense Donald Rumsfeld and National Security Adviser Condoleezza Rice into the presence of Tim Russert and George Will, Secretary of State Colin Powell to the World Economic Forum in Davos, Switzerland, on January 26, 2003, and then on February 5 to the United Nations Security Council.

The news media provided fanfares of loyal support. The no-nonsense cover lines on the *New York Times Magazine* for January 5 ("The American Empire, Get Used to It") were

matched by the brass-band rhetoric of the lead article written by Michael Ignatieff, a brand-name foreign policy intellectual recruited from the faculty of Harvard:

> Imperial powers do not have the luxury of timidity, for
> timidity is not prudence; it is a confession of weak-
> ness. . . .

> [The United States] remain[s] a nation in which flag, sacri-
> fice, and martial honor are central to national identity. . . .

> Americans are required, even when they are unwilling to
> do so, to include Europeans in the governance of their
> evolving imperial project. The Americans essentially dictate
> Europe's place in this new grand design. The United States
> is multilateral when it wants to be, unilateral when it must
> be; and it enforces a new division of labor in which Amer-
> ica does the fighting, the French, British and Germans do
> the police patrols in the border zones and the Dutch,
> Swiss and Scandinavians provide the humanitarian aid.

Ignatieff briefly raised the question of terminology (America as democratic republic, America as military empire) but
then went on to say that it doesn't make much difference
how America chooses to name or see itself. The words
don't matter. The country is what it is, so rich and powerful
and good that it can't help but do what is just and right
and true. America, the world's unrivaled hegemon, an empire

in fact if not in name, its sovereign power the only hope for less fortunate nations groping toward the light of free markets and liberal democracy. Be not timid, do not flinch. Shoulder the burden of civilization and its discontents. Lift from the continents of Africa and Asia the weight of despotic evildoers. Know that if Americans do the fighting, other people will do the dying.

In concert with Ignatieff's marching song, *Newsweek* discovered in President Bush the character of "a warrior king . . . comfortable in ermine," and the bestselling hagiographies hurried into print by Bob Woodward (*Bush at War*) and David Frum (*The Right Man*) poured forth phrases perfumed with myrrh and frankincense—"steely, eye-of-storm serenity," "casting his mission and that of the country in the grand vision of God's master plan," "impervious to doubt." Every newspaper in the country welcomed Secretary Powell's performance at the United Nations with corroborating sighs of helpless infatuation. The secretary held up air force surveillance photographs requiring the same kind of arcane exposition that New York art critics attach to exhibitions of abstract painting, displayed a vial of white powder (meant to be seen as anthrax but closer in its chemistry to granulated sugar), and rolled tape of two satellite telephone intercepts of Iraqi military officers screaming at each other in Arabic. The theatrical effects evaded an answer to the question, Why does America attack Iraq when Iraq hasn't attacked America? In lieu of demonstrable provocations Mr. Powell offered disturbing signs and evil portents, and when the voice of

Osama bin Laden turned up a week later on an audiotape broadcast from Qatar, the secretary seized upon the occasion to discover a "partnership" between Al Qaeda and the government of Iraq. No such conclusion could be drawn from even a careless reading of the transcript, but to Mr. Powell the sending of a message (any message) proved that Osama bin Laden and Saddam Hussein had somehow morphed into the same enemy. The secretary's power points didn't add to the sum of a convincing argument, but then neither had the advertising copy for the Spanish-American War or the sales promotions for the war in Vietnam, and if the agitprop failed to persuade the French, Russian, or Chinese representatives to the Security Council, it was more than good enough for the emissaries from the major American news media.*

The absence of institutional opposition to the American war policy eventually provoked dissenting street protests not only in the United States but also among large numbers of people elsewhere in the world, with massive public demonstrations on February 15 taking place in more than six hun-

---

*In an op-ed piece for the *Washington Post,* Gilbert Cranberg (professor emeritus at the University of Iowa's school of journalism) drew from the media's response to Powell's slide show a lesson in credulity: "An examination of a mix of some forty papers from all parts of the country, shows that while some were less convinced than others by Powell's attempt to link Hussein to terrorism, there was unanimity as to Iraq's possession of weapons of mass destruction: 'a massive array of evidence,' 'a detailed and persuasive case,' 'a powerful case,' 'a sober factual case,' 'an overwhelming case,' 'a compelling case,' 'the strong, credible and persuasive case,' 'a persuasive detailed accumulation of information,' 'the core of

dred cities across all twenty-four time zones and drawing crowds of 250,000 people in New York, 750,000 in London, 1.3 million in Barcelona. The major media dismissed the uproar as one of little worth and no consequence—the work of aging flower children and B-list Hollywood celebrities; President Bush likened it to the assembling of an ad agency's hired focus group, an expression of nonserious and uninformed opinion not apt to affect his judgment, alter his course of action, or trespass in the temple of his unilateral enlightenment. Three weeks later, when he appeared in the White House on the evening of March 6 to announce the imminent scourging of Iraq, it was a wonder that he didn't speak in tongues. His topic was secular but his message was sacred, the blank expression engraved on his face disquietingly similar to the thousand-yard stare of the true believer gazing into the mirror of eternity. Answering questions for the better part of an hour from the assembled scribes and Pharisees, the president bore witness to a revelation mounted on four pillars of holy wrath:

---

his argument was unassailable,' 'a smoking fusillade . . . a persuasive case for anyone who is still persuadable,' 'an accumulation of painstakingly gathered and analyzed evidence,' 'only the most gullible and wishful thinking souls can now deny that Iraq is harboring and hiding weapons of mass destruction,' 'the skeptics asked for proof; they now have it,' 'a much more detailed and convincing argument than any that has previously been told,' 'Powell's evidence . . . was overwhelming,' 'an ironclad case . . . incontrovertible evidence,' 'succinct and damning evidence . . . the case is closed,' 'Colin Powell delivered the goods on Saddam Hussein,' 'masterful,' 'If there was any doubt that Hussein needs to be . . . stripped of his chemical and biological capabilities, Powell put it to rest.'"

1. America allies itself with Christ and goes to war to rid the world of evil.
2. Iraq is Sodom, or possibly Gomorrah.
3. Saddam is the Devil's spawn.
4. Any nation refusing to join the "coalition of the willing" deserves to perish in the deserts of disbelief.*

If during the months prior to the bombing of Baghdad on March 19, every government spokesperson in Washington had attributed to Saddam Hussein the supernatural powers of the Antichrist, the first week of the invasion proved every assertion false. In place of Adolf Hitler or Joseph Stalin (a villain "stifling the world," presenting an immediate and terrible danger not only to the peoples of Saudi Arabia, Israel, and Kuwait but also to every man, woman, and child in the United States, certain to oppose any attempts of punishment with vengeful clouds of poison gas), the American armies found remnants of a dictator more accurately compared to a psychopathic prison warden, a brutal but almost comic figure, so enslaved by the dream of his omnipotence

---

*The president knows himself allied with the thrones of Christian virtue, and if left to his own or to his speechwriters' devices in front of an open microphone, he seldom misses a chance to restate the good news in the language of the Bible: "The liberty we prize is not America's gift to the world; it is God's gift to humanity." "We do not claim to know all the ways of Providence, yet we can trust in them, placing our confidence in the loving God behind all life, and all of history." "Events aren't moved by blind change and chance . . . [but] by the hand of a just and faithful God." "We will export death and violence to the four corners of the earth in defense of our great nation."

that he apparently had entrusted the defense of his kingdom to histrionic press releases and gigantic portraits of himself armed with a shotgun and a porkpie hat. No Iraqi shock troops appeared in the field to oppose the Third Infantry Division's advance into the valley of the Euphrates; no Iraqi aircraft presumed to leave the ground; no allied combat unit met with, much less knew where to find, the fabled weapons of mass destruction. The desultory shows of resistance at the river crossings constituted ragged skirmish lines of young men for the most part poorly armed, so many of them out of uniform that it wasn't worth the trouble to distinguish between the military and the civilian dead.

The weakness of the Iraqi target made ridiculous Washington's propaganda posters. Here was the American army in the sinister landscape of Iraq, equipped to fight the Battle of Normandy or El Alamein but conducting a police action in the manner of the Israeli assassination teams hunting down Palestinian terrorists in the rubble of the Gaza Strip. How then would it be possible to hide in plain sight the false pretext of Operation Iraqi Freedom? The Bush administration answered the question by simply changing the mission statement. The American army had not come to Iraq to remove the totalitarian menace threatening all of Western civilization—absolutely not; the American army had come briefly eastward into Eden to "liberate" the long-suffering Iraqi people from the misery inflicted upon them by an evildoer with the bad habit of cutting out their tongues. One excuse for war was as good as any other.

The cable networks meanwhile rejoiced in the chance to

tell a tale worthy of the late Stephen Ambrose's *Band of Brothers* and Tom Brokaw's *The Greatest Generation.* Journalists on duty at the Pentagon characterized the assault as a magnificent achievement, one of the most extraordinary military campaigns ever conducted in the history of the world; reporters traveling with the troops discovered comparisons to the glory of World War II—the tanks in the desert reminding them of Generals George Patton and Erwin Rommel, the Siege of Basra analogous to the defense of Stalingrad. When temporarily short of incoming footage from Iraq, the television producers in Washington and New York dressed up their screens with American flags and courageous anchorpersons pledging allegiance to "America's Bravest." MSNBC decorated its primary set with a portrait of President Bush—the studio equivalent of a loyalty oath—and the executive in charge of the network was proud to say that the press had no business asking ugly questions. "After September 11 the country wants more optimism and benefit of the doubt. . . . It's about being positive as opposed to being negative." At Fox News the talking heads transformed their jingoistic fervor into an article of totalitarian faith, their on-camera sermons preached directly to any scoundrels who might have wandered into the viewing audience with the dissenting notion that the war was not a war and therefore unnecessary as well as wrong: "You were sickening then, you are sickening now," "leftist stooges," "absolutely committing sedition, or treason."

Although by Easter Sunday the purification of Iraq was still a work in progress—Saddam Hussein nowhere to be found, sporadic gunfire lingering in the streets of Baghdad and Mosul, a new government not yet seated on its prayer rugs—in Washington the flags were blooming on the bandstands, and the heralds of American empire were crying up the news of great and glorious victory. The legions under the command of General Tommy Franks had destroyed the semblance of an Iraqi army, rescued the oil fields of Kirkuk, chased an evil tyrant from his throne, cleansed the cradle of civilization of an unsanitary regime. Priced at the cost of $60 billion and 129 American lives (45 of them lost in accidents), the month's work lifted President George W. Bush to a 70 percent approval rating in the opinion polls, the friends and officers of his administration everywhere attended by congratulatory nods and gifts of loyal applause. Important newspaper columnists pointed proudly to the "high-water mark" of America's "resurgent power"; elevated sources at the White House declared themselves well pleased with "the demonstration effect" of a military maneuver that "opens all sorts of new opportunities for us."

Concerns about the possible squeamishness of the prime-time audience when exposed to scenes of horror proved to be unwarranted and overblown. On the first day of hostilities President Bush cautioned the country's senior news executives against publishing photographs of dead Iraqi civilians. As events moved forward and the home audience registered its approval of a new and improved form of reality TV, it was understood that foreign dead counted merely as unpaid extras briefly available to the producers of the nightly news to fuel the fireballs and stand around in front of the machine-gun bullets. By April 12 the American public had shown sufficient bravery in the face of a distant enemy that the *New York Times* didn't think it imprudent to publish a handsome color photograph of dead Iraqi children thrown like spoiled vegetables into a refrigerated truck.

But if the pictures didn't present a problem, one still had to be careful with the words. As a matter of well-known and long-established principle, imperialist powers shoot and kill only for the good of the people shot down, but the policy usually requires some sort of upbeat euphemism ("the training of backward peoples" in the art of "democratic self-government") with which to ease the minds of the women and children in the room. The producers of the March on Baghdad took the necessary precautions. The killing of Iraqis, both military and civilian, was softened to "attriting" or "degrading" resources; when it was noticed that in Arabic the word "fedayeen" means "those who sacrifice themselves for a cause," our official spokesmen substituted "terrorist death squads"; the looting of the Iraqi National Museum and the burning of the country's National Library were ascribed to the joys of "freedom." Nothing to do with our navy's cruise missiles, of course, and in no way the fault of our army units that had neglected to protect both buildings, and with them the twelve-thousand-year history of a civilization that prior to the arrival of General Franks had survived the conquests of the Byzantine emperor Heraclius, Suleiman the Magnificent, and Genghis Khan. Secretary of Defense Donald Rumsfeld scowled at the suggestion that somehow the destruction could have been prevented, possibly in the same way that American troops preserved the Oil Ministry. "Freedom's untidy," he said, "and free people are free to make mistakes and commit crimes and do bad things."

So are military empires free to seize "all sorts of new opportunities" opened to them by "demonstration effects" similar to the ones brought by an Athenian army to the island of Melos in the summer of 416 B.C. Having first butchered the Melian military commanders, the Athenians presented the citizens of the town with the choice of abandoning their loyalty to Sparta or accepting the sentence of death.

"As practical men," said the Athenian heralds, "you know and we know that the question of justice arises only between parties equal in strength, and the strong do what they can, and the weak submit."

The corporate managers of the Bush administration lack the concision of the Attic style, but they didn't find it hard to appreciate the ancient moral of the tale. The high-tech gladiatorial show in the Iraqi colosseum had served as a test market not only for the Pentagon's new and exciting inventory of weapons but also for the premise of American military empire—established the necessary precedent, set the proper tone, opened the road to the grandeur that was Rome. Heartened by the message delivered to the voters in the next American presidential election as well as to America's enemies both east and west of Suez, various staff officers attached to the White House, its supporting neoconservative think tanks, and the Pentagon expressed varying degrees of satisfaction. Secretary of State Colin Powell threatened Syria, telling a press conference that Syria would have to change its ways, but, no, there was "no war plan right now." Vice President Dick Cheney admonished Germany and France, indicating that neither country could expect oil or construction contracts from a new jurisdiction in Iraq, saying that "perhaps time will help in terms of improving their outlook." Ken Adelman, a member of the Pentagon's Defense Policy Board, hoped that the conquest of Baghdad "emboldens leaders to drastic, not measured, approaches"; Michael Ledeen, resident scholar in the Freedom Chair at the American Enterprise Institute, placed the great victory in geopolitical perspective: "Every ten years or so, the United States needs to pick up some crappy little country and throw it against the wall, just to show the world we mean business."

Thus spake the Zarathustras of the Bush administration contemplating the ruin of what was once the World Trade Center. Let any nation anywhere on earth even begin to think of challenging the American supremacy (military, cultural, socioeconomic), and America reserves the right to strangle the impudence at birth—to bomb the peasants or the palace, block the flows of oil or bank credit, change the linen in the information ministries and the hotels. The motion carried without undue objection on the part of the American public or the American news media. Told that the truth didn't matter, that motive was irrelevant, and that the Bush administration was free to do as it pleased, the heirs and assigns of what was once a democratic republic greeted the announcement with an audible and respectful silence.

TWO
Gag Rule

War is the health of the state.

—RANDOLPH BOURNE

As a cure for the distemper of a restive electorate and a stop in the mouth of a possibly quarrelsome press, nothing works as well as the lollipop of a foreign war. The dodge is as old as chariots in Egypt, but by the autumn of 2003, the Bush administration had little else with which to demonstrate either the goodness of its heart or the worth of its existence. The oracles at CBS and CNN weren't as yet foreseeing a regime change in Washington after the election of 2004, but the president was losing the confidence of the opinion polls (an approval rating of 76 percent in April, 50 percent on November 1), the economy mortgaged to a federal debt roughly estimated at $7 trillion, another 2.5 million Americans enlisted in the army of the terminally impoverished, and the price of glory in Iraq proving to be somewhat higher than previously supposed—210 American soldiers killed since the war was said to have ended its theatrical run in May, the occupation costing $4 billion instead of $2 billion a month, Saddam not yet dead or captured, no weapons of mass destruction anywhere in sight.

The acknowledgment in early July of the president's misstatement about Saddam's acquisition of African uranium prompted the members of Washington's political theater company to strike strong poses of indignation and dismay, to call for congressional investigations and bat the tennis balls of blame around the Sunday talk-show circuit. Even the major news media were beginning to ask whether the Bush administration had been telling the truth about its reasons for bringing the wonders of democracy to Baghdad, and among the prospective candidates for the Democratic name on the next presidential ballot, the strongest surge of money and applause was flowing toward Howard Dean, a former governor of Vermont chiefly distinguished by his willingness to portray George W. Bush as a liar and a fool.

The president countered any and all criticisms with the generous pouring out of patriotic sentiment. Throughout the months of September and October he chose to speak whenever possible at military bases, and he seldom failed to strike the note of "The Battle Hymn of the Republic," urging Christian soldiers forward on their march into the deserts of godless barbarism. From the White House on September 7, his lectern and seal of office placed in the Cabinet Room under the portrait of Thomas Jefferson, the president asked Congress for another $87 billion to finance the great cause of freedom in Afghanistan and Iraq, and by so doing to guarantee the life and liberty of the American people. For America, he said, "there will be no going back to the era before September 11, 2001, to false comfort in a dangerous world . . . we are fighting the enemy in Iraq and Afghanistan today so that we do not meet them again on our own streets, in our own cities."*

Three days later at the FBI training academy in Quantico, Virginia, the president told a cheering crowd of federal investigators that the homeland defense against terrorism must be reinforced with "administrative subpoenas" unhindered by the niggling inconvenience of a court order. "No terrorist networks," he said, "will ever gain weapons of mass destruction from Saddam Hussein's regime. That regime is no more."† On September 27 at United Nations headquarters in New York, Mr. Bush reminded the members of the General Assembly of the higher "moral law" that must guide the actions of all men and all governments confronted with "the war against civilization." Some of the countries represented in the hall, most notably Germany and France, had shown a distinct lack of properly martial spirit prior to the American invasion of Iraq, but now the time had come for them to "earn the favorable judgment of history," to

---

*The same line of false reasoning, under the label "the Domino Theory," sponsored the American debacle in Vietnam. The Senate passed the requested legislation on October 17 by a vote of 87 to 12, adding the $87 billion to the $79 billion already appropriated in May to pay the initial costs of the Iraq expedition.
†No terrorist organizations ever did gain weapons of mass destruction from Saddam Hussein. Saddam had none to give.

realign themselves with the forces of truth and justice, and join, wholeheartedly, the battle in which "there is no neutral ground."*

While the president was appearing on national television to bang the drum of war and muster the constituencies of fear, Vice President Dick Cheney and Secretary of Defense Donald Rumsfeld appeared before smaller and more select audiences to defend the administration's policy against the objections of watery idealists, weak minded and misinformed. Before an audience of supportive policy intellectuals at the Heritage Foundation in Washington, Mr. Cheney scorned the critics who suggested that the threat posed by Saddam Hussein was in no way imminent. "Since when have terrorists and tyrants announced their intentions, politely putting us on notice before they strike. . . . Had we followed the counsel of inaction, the Iraqi regime would still be a menace to its neighbors and a destabilizing force in the Middle East. Today, because we acted, Iraq stands to be a force for good in the Middle East." At the Ronald Reagan Library and Museum in Simi Valley, California, Secretary Rumsfeld attributed the impression of failure to the bias of the liberal news media. "The part of the picture that's negative is being

---

*Three weeks before the Nazi invasion of Poland in the summer of 1939, Adolf Hitler presented the German general staff with a similarly brave choice: "The victor will not be asked afterwards whether he told the truth or not. In starting and waging a war, it is not right that matters, but victory."

emphasized," he said, "and the part of the picture that's positive is not."*

Attorney General John Ashcroft meanwhile was touring the country to count the blessings of the USA PATRIOT Act, recently strengthened with the definition of the newly minted crime of "domestic terrorism" as "any action that endangers human life or is a violation of any federal or state law." A transgression so broadly defined allows for so many interpretations, many of them fanciful and most of them abusive, that the Justice Department was attaching the label of terrorism to its investigations of drug traffickers, money launderers, and child pornographers. The antidemocratic

---

*In August 2002, advising his deputy, Paul Wolfowitz, on the proper way to answer possibly irksome questions at Pentagon press conferences, Rumsfeld said: "Begin with an illogical premise and proceed, perfectly logically, to the illogical conclusion." Two months earlier, in Brussels for a meeting of the NATO allies, the secretary had set a particularly fine example of the correct approach. To a crowd of reporters asking about the progress of the war on terrorism, he delivered a speech worthy of the riddling fool in one of Shakespeare's enchanted forests:

> The message is that there are no "knowns." There are things we know that we know. There are known unknowns. That is to say there are things that we now know we don't know. But there are also unknown unknowns. There are things we don't know we don't know. So when we do the best we can and we pull all this information together, and we then say well that's basically what we see as the situation, that is really only the known knowns and the known unknowns. And each year, we discover a few more of those unknown unknowns. . . . There's another way to phrase that and that is that the absence of evidence is not evidence of absence.

premise of the legislation had provoked complaints across the whole of the political spectrum—from senators both liberal and conservative, from members of the National Rifle Association as well as members of the American Civil Liberties Union. The shows of unruliness offended the attorney general. Undertaking to defend the purposes of the PATRIOT Act, he scheduled appearances in sixteen states deemed important to the president's winning the election of 2004. His message was invariably one of impending doom—the continuing bloodshed in the streets of Baghdad indicative of terrorists lurking under the Brooklyn Bridge, driving bomb-laden trucks north to Boston, south to Tallahassee; if America was to be kept safe from further harm, then the laws must become more vigilant, not less. People who said otherwise were feeble minded and disloyal, "soft on terrorism," ignoring the lesson of September 11.*

Ashcroft took particular care to stress the latter point when his travels brought him to Federal Hall in Lower Manhattan, not far from the place where Congress met in 1789 to adopt

---

*Ashcroft was especially annoyed by an amendment passed by the House of Representatives in July, by a vote of 309 to 118, that limited the Justice Department's use of "sneak and peek" warrants. The amendment's sponsor, Representative C. L. Otter (R.-Idaho), had argued that the provision granted the Justice Department a license to make random and arbitrary searches. Ashcroft described the amendment as "a mistake . . . the members didn't know what they were voting for." Offended by the dismissive tone of the remark, Charles Eberle, also a Republican congressman from Idaho, said, "Ashcroft wants more power . . . what a lot of us in Idaho are saying is, 'Let's not get rid of the checks and balances.' . . . We don't like the government intruding on our constitutional rights."

the Bill of Rights and close enough to Ground Zero to furnish the setting for a heroic photo op. Framed by marble columns, against a backdrop of American flags, Ashcroft spoke to an invited audience of law enforcement officials seated attentively in a semicircle of folding chairs. The proceeding was closed to the public, no possibly seditious spectators permitted in the balcony or the rotunda. Like Cheney in Washington, Ashcroft in New York refused to suffer the indignity of questions. Too many Americans, he said, had forgotten the "shock, anger, grief and anguish" of the awful September morning when death came to Wall Street from a blue and cloudless sky. Such people needed to be brought to attention, taught to appreciate the watchfulness of a government always looking out for their spiritual and moral welfare as well as for their physical safety. Overly liberal complainants wishing to remove or amend some of the more repressive strictures of the PATRIOT Act were unwitting dupes of a foreign power—not quite traitors, at least not yet, but dangerously slack in the performance of their duties to the state. Asked to address the concern raised by librarians required to turn over lists of books borrowed by any reader whom the Justice Department cared to name (the librarian under legal obligation not to inform the reader of the government's interest), Ashcroft said, "baseless hysteria . . . why would the FBI care how far you have gotten in the latest Tom Clancy novel."

Despite the government's incessant crying up of its global war on terror, President Bush's approval ratings continued to drift downward with the leaves of autumn. Every evening's television broadcast brought word of another American sol-

dier killed in Iraq by a land mine or a grenade, another building blown up by another car bomb, another Iraqi police official assassinated for the crime of collaborating with the
American occupation. The accumulation of bad news brought
President Bush to the podium of a hastily summoned press
conference in the White House Rose Garden on October 28,
his rare appearance before a civilian audience inspired by a
series of suicide bombings that during the preceding three
days had killed forty people in Baghdad—four American
military, thirty-six Iraqi civilian. The president parsed the violence as testimony to the success of America's democracy
project, evidence of the "desperation" on the part of freedom's enemies (diehard followers of Saddam Hussein, terrorist agents imported from Syria and Iran) seeking to delay
the inevitable triumph of justice by weakening the will to
"stay the course." Although careful not to put the sophism in
words too plainly understood, the president was saying that
the more good people who died in Iraq (Americans, Iraqis,
Red Cross nurses, UN relief workers), the more it was a sign
that we were winning the fight against the bad people in Iraq.
The more dangerous the streets of Baghdad, the safer the
streets in Columbus, Ohio. "I think the American people are
patient during an election year," the president said, "because
they tend to be able to differentiate between, you know, politics and reality."*

---

*Rush Limbaugh had made a similar point about the good news from Iraq in an
August radio broadcast to the Republican faithful. It was a wonderful thing, he
said, that so many terrorists had come to Baghdad. They presented themselves as

The news media assembled on the lawn were grateful for the reassurance, and with very few prominent exceptions they contented themselves, as did the loyal majorities in both houses of Congress, with mild admonishments—yes, the country's intelligence agencies were at fault, but, under the circumstances, the mistakes were understandable; yes, the Pentagon apparently hadn't given much thought to the long-term consequences of Operation Iraqi Freedom, but now that America had come to Baghdad, how could we abandon the noble enterprise? New bridges were being built across the Tigris River; shipments of food and medicine were arriving in Samarra and Mosul; the coalition forces might be experiencing technical difficulties with sporadic gunfire, but while the rescue of Iraq was still a work in progress, impertinent questions from the news media betrayed a lack of sensitivity to the plight of the Iraqi people, formerly enslaved, now free to elect any imam who promised not to slit their throats. The arsenal of the apocalypse never was the only reason for the advance into the valley of the Euphrates (merely one of many reasons, the others too subtle or abstract to explain to the prime-time television audience), and the world was well rid of Saddam Hussein no matter what the pretext for his departure.

This provisional opinion earned promotion to certain fact on December 13, when the U.S. Army's Fourth Infantry Division found Saddam underneath a farmhouse ten miles

---

easier and more obvious targets. "We don't have to go anywhere to find them!" he said. "They've fielded a Jihad All-Star Team."

south of Tikrit. The triumphant film footage transformed the once defiant villain into an enfeebled vagrant, unshaven and lice infested, looking to his captors "like a rat in a hole." Thirty-six hours later at a happily convened White House press conference, President Bush acknowledged the humiliation of his enemy with the same phrase—"when the heat got on, you dug yourself a hole and you crawled into it . . . good riddance, the world is better without you."

The capture of Saddam instantly reinvigorated the president's approval ratings in the opinion polls (up by 10 percentage points over the span of two days) and strengthened his persona as a commander in chief skilled in the arts of militant diplomacy. The good news from abroad coincided with good news at home—Congress granted a Medicare prescription drug benefit in the amount of $400 billion; the Dow Jones Industrial Average rose above 10,000 points for the first time in nearly two years. To further buttress the image of the Bush administration as that of the country's Great and Good Protector, the Department of Homeland Security on December 21 declared a state of high terror alert for the Christmas holidays, canceling several flights on foreign airlines arriving from Britain, France, and Mexico and posting Black Hawk helicopters over Times Square on New Year's Eve.

The combination of circumstances served to quiet the mutterings of the news media and to confuse the contenders for the Democratic presidential nomination. The front-running candidate, Howard Dean, continued to insist on his objection to the government policy of preemptive strike (the capture of Saddam, he said, "did not make America safer"), but the other would-be leaders of the Democratic Party, among them Senators Joseph Lieberman and John Kerry, raised questions about Dean's overly pungent rhetoric and cast doubt on his "electability"; not wishing to give or take offense, they searched for the safer politics of loyal consensus. Support the troops, vote the money, pray for miracles, and in time of trouble don't speak harshly of the country's rulers.*

The same sales pitch maintained the policies of Nazi Germany and imperial Rome. Nor has it been unknown in the history of the United States, the power points amended and revised to match the shifting definition of what was seen to constitute "the national security." The God-fearing congregations of colonial New England believed themselves threatened by witches, and the luckless women so identified were hanged as enemies of the state. The first newspaper ever published in the American colonies, *Publick Occurrences*

---

*Among the few newspaper columnists who didn't swallow the story, Paul Krugman in the *New York Times* remarked on the government's gift for "systematically" and "brazenly distorting the facts to an extent never before seen in U.S. history." Krugman went on to say, "Suppose that this administration did con us into war. And suppose that it is not held accountable for its deceptions . . . in that case, our political system has become utterly, perhaps irrevocably, corrupted." Similar observations showed up in the pages of *The Nation* and *The Progressive*, also on *The Daily Show* with Jon Stewart and in a number of briefly bestselling books, among them Al Franken's *Lies and the Lying Liars Who Tell Them: A Fair and Balanced Look at the Right*, Molly Ivins and Lou Dubose's *Bushwhacked*, Joe Conason's *Big Lies*, Jim Hightower's *Thieves in High Places*, and Krugman's own *The Great Unraveling*. Although often well taken and to the point, the dissenting remarks were marketed and sold as harmless entertainment.

Both Foreign and Domestick, appeared in Boston in 1690, its purpose, as defined by its printer, Benjamin Harris, "to cure the spirit of lying much among us." The British authorities shut down the paper after one edition on the grounds that printer Harris hadn't applied for a license to publish.

The Sedition Act passed by the Federalist Congress in 1798 prohibited "any false, scandalous and malicious writing . . . against the government of the United States, or President of the United States, with intent to defame said government (or Congress or President) with intent to bring them into contempt or disrepute, or to excite against them the hatred of the good people of the United States." The law derived from the country's fear of being goaded into the Napoleonic Wars, and the severity of the punishments imposed for its breach (heavy fines, two years in prison) reflected the impassioned state of American political feeling at a time when merchant ships sailing from Boston and New York were being seized by both the French and British navies.

In the streets of Philadelphia, then serving as the nation's capital, Federalists wearing in their hats the black cockades expressive of their sympathy for Britain hurled stones and insults at the Republicans wearing the red-white-and-blue caps of liberty, signifying support for France. President Adams proclaimed the need for an American monarchy and issued a summons for five thousand militia to enforce the opinion given voice in *Porcupine's Gazette:* "If Jefferson had his way, the country would see the Bible cast into a bonfire . . . our wives and daughters the victims of legal prostitution, our sons the disciples of Voltaire, and the dragoons of Marat."

The *Gazette* favored the Federalist side of the argument, and its editor, William Cobbett, writing under the name Peter Porcupine, disdained any and all professions of impartiality. "They are always useless," he said, "and are besides perfect nonsense, when used by a newsmonger; for, he that does not relate news as he finds it, is something worse than partial and . . . he that does not exercise his own judgment, either in admitting or rejecting what is sent him, is a poor passive tool, and not an editor." Cobbett directed his best and brightest slander at Benjamin Bache, the grandson of Benjamin Franklin, the editor of the Republican newspaper the *Aurora,* and a man in whom the *Gazette* found no sign of saving grace: "All the world knows and says he is a liar; a fallen wretch, a vessel formed for reprobation, and therefore we should always treat him as we would a TURK, a JEW, a JACOBIN or a DOG." Unlike our own nominally outspoken journalists, Bache wasn't shy about returning the insults. The *Aurora* routinely referred to the president of the United States as "old, bald, blind, querulous, toothless, crippled John Adams," to the Federalists as apprentice tyrants wearing the same mask of rank hypocrisy worn by "a CAESAR, a CROMWELL and a WASHINGTON."*

A contentious and rabble-rousing tone of voice continued to enliven American newspapers throughout the early nineteenth century, as many as a thousand of them by 1840

---

*Jefferson's first term in office didn't result in the revolutionary upheaval foretold by the friends of Alexander Hamilton and George III, and the Sedition Act was revoked in 1801—soon enough to allow for the public scourging of Aaron Burr, but not before twenty-five editors had been arrested and Bache had died in prison.

advancing vigorous if often bigoted opinions from all points on the political compass—for the abolition of slavery, against the arrival of European immigrants, in favor of massacring the Plains Indians, opposed to women's suffrage or the establishment of a national bank. The expanding sense of national purpose associated with the waging of both the Mexican and Civil Wars muffled the expressions of dissent in the more popular assumption that America was destined to become, in the words of a characteristic speech delivered in Covington, Kentucky, on July 4, 1850, by William Evans Arthur, apprentice congressman and judge, "the ark of safety, the anointed civilizer, the only visible source of light and heat and repose in a dark and discordant and troubled world."

Abraham Lincoln at different intervals in his career allied himself with each side of the story. As a young congressman from Illinois in 1846, he opposed the theory of "Manifest Destiny" justifying the invasion of Mexico for reasons that he subsequently explained to William Herndon, his erstwhile law partner: "Allow the President to invade a neighboring nation whenever he shall deem it necessary to repel an invasion . . . and you allow him to make war at pleasure. . . . [I]f today he should choose to say that he thinks it necessary to invade Canada to prevent the British from invading us, how could you stop him? You may say to him, 'I see no probability of the British invading us,' but he would say to you, 'Be silent: I see it if you don't.' "

As president during the Civil War, seeking to preserve a

union "conceived in Liberty and dedicated to the proposition that all men are created equal," Lincoln occasionally suspended the right of habeas corpus and ordered the imprisonment of several thousand civilians suspected of making careless, offhand remarks critical of his policy. Not surprisingly, the Civil War fostered the suppression of disagreeable opinion in every arena of American politics, in the chambers of Congress as well as in newspapers north of Baltimore and south of Richmond, but it was the applications of the gag rule by the McKinley and Wilson administrations around the turn of the twentieth century that established the precedents for those currently being put to use by the Bush administration. If by 1890 the Industrial Revolution had made America rich, so also had it alerted the electorate to the unequal division of the spoils. People had begun to notice the loaded dice in the hands of the railroad and banking monopolies, the tax burden shifting from capital to labor. A severe depression in the winter of 1893–94 brought with it widespread unemployment, vicious strikes in the Pennsylvania steel mills and the West Virginia coal mines, hobo armies on the march in the Ohio Valley and the Appalachian Mountains. The demand for social and political reform prompted the angry stirring of a populist movement across the prairies of the Middle West, and the threatened loss of political control obliged the nervous oligarchies of the monied East to find, in the words of an alarmed U.S. senator, "something" to knock the "pus" out of this "anarchistic, socialistic and populistic boil." The McKinley administration came up with war in Cuba, the conquest of the Philippines, the annexation of Puerto Rico, and what was known as a "large" foreign policy deemed "essential to the greatness of every splendid people," necessary "to the strength and dignity of any nation." How better to muzzle the republican spirit and replace the love of liberty with the love of the flag than with the trappings of imperial grandeur—every true American a patriot, all political quarrels to be suspended in the interest of "the national security."*

Perceived by Henry Adams as "easily first in genius for manipulation . . . an uncommonly dangerous politician," McKinley during the 1896 election campaign posed as an enemy of the eastern monied interests and never once mentioned the word Cuba. As soon as he was settled in the White House, he declared his sympathy for Wall Street and discovered that it was impossible to ignore "the cries of outraged humanity" wafting across the Straits of Florida on every

---

*The mechanics of the exchange provided the late Walter Karp with the topic of *The Politics of War,* a book published in 1979 but one that offers a better understanding of our present political circumstance than most of the commentary paraded out of Washington since the advent of the Reagan administration. Karp's passion was politics, and his precepts were simple and few. Taking his cue from Thomas Paine, he made a clear distinction between the American Republic and the American nation—"deadly rivals for the love and loyalty of the American people." Always mistrustful of what he called the "official version" of things, Karp professed his allegiance to the republic; the nation he regarded as a poor, dim thing, assembled as a corporate entity, sustained by an "artificial patriotism," and given the semblance of meaning only when puffed up with the excitements of a foreign war.

southern breeze. Aware that the American people would not have supported an honestly advertised program of overseas conquest, McKinley also knew that they might accept, albeit uneasily, the gift of an accidental empire. His agents in Congress voted money to nonexistent but supposedly beleaguered Cuban revolutionaries, the State Department issued ultimatums to the supposedly evildoing government of Spain, and the New York newspapers printed sensational stories from nonexistent correspondents in Cuba describing "bloodshed on the island more than the human heart can bear." Thus overwhelmed by "Happenstance" and "The Will of Providence," the seemingly reluctant McKinley ("We must follow duty even if desire opposes") led the country into a war that countered no foreign threat, secured no national economic advantage, and served only to preserve the Republican oligarchy's hold on power.

By the time President Theodore Roosevelt moved his cavalry horses into the White House stables in 1901, the last remnants of populist unrest had drifted into the sunset with the wreckage of the Spanish fleet, and for the next five years the agents and apostles of the American nation gloried in a triumph of wealth and cynicism presumed sufficient to silence any loose-mouthed talk about ordinary citizens deserving a say in a government nominally democratic. That presumption soon collapsed under the weight of its complaisance and stupidity. Incapable of managing an economy that it could only prey upon, "the money power" and its hired politicians consigned the arrangement of the country's financial affairs to a consortium of swindling bankers and bribed legislatures. Not unlike the bandmasters of the Bush administration, the tribunes of the people at the zenith of the country's Gilded Age embraced the view of Senator Nelson Aldrich of Rhode Island, who regarded any kind of politics save the politics of corrupt privilege as "sentimental rot."

During the first decade of the twentieth century the continuing proofs of the oligarchy's disdain for such a thing as the common good translated the resentments once lodged in the rural counties of populist discontent into the clamor of the progressive movement. Awakened to a sense of political and economic injustice by the muckraking journalism of the day, the urban middle classes seconded the motion for a change of system, and against a more sophisticated enemy, the friends of the protective tariff and Yankee Doodle Dandy had need of more strenuous countermeasures. They found their salvation in the hypocrisy of Woodrow Wilson, who engineered America's entry into World War I in order to damp down the fevers of domestic discontent. Just as Operation Iraqi Freedom was not about the rescue of the Iraqi people, so also the Spanish-American War was not about "the sacred cause of Cuban independence," and our entry into World War I not about keeping the world "safe for democracy." Presidents McKinley and Wilson sought to punish foreign crimes against humanity, the ones committed by villains in Havana and Brussels, in order to make America safe for the domestic crimes against humanity committed by the top-hatted gentlemen in Cleveland, Chicago, and New York.

Although Wilson, like McKinley, had campaigned for the White House on the promise of social reform, he betrayed his presumed principles at the earliest opportunity. Within a matter of weeks after taking office, in the spring of 1913, Wilson discovered it his "unavoidable duty" to send the U.S. Marines to Mexico to overthrow the renegade and evildoing regime of Victoriano Huerta and thus "to teach the Mexicans to elect good men." Soon after the outbreak of war in Europe, Wilson wrote a letter to the editor of the *New York Times* saying that all true Americans could now look back, "as if upon a bad dream," at the years of their dissension and unrest. "The legislation of the past year and a half," he said, "has remedied all of the people's just grievances. The era of reform, a period of dangerous ill humors and distempers now thankfully at an end. A terrible dozen years when those who had power, whether in business or in politics, were almost universally looked upon with suspicion." A year later, drumming up enthusiasm for America's engagement in World War I, Wilson called upon the nation to rebuke the voices of disagreement, drown out dissent with the "deep unison of the common, unhesitatingly national feeling . . . let us lift up our eyes to the great tracts of life yet to be conquered in the interests of our righteous peace."

The emergence of the United States as a world power between the years 1890 and 1920 followed from the domestic political crisis threatening to remove control of the country's wealth and well-being from the custody of its newly ascendant ruling class—the passions of war meant to overrule the motion for economic justice, the band music intended to silence the solo voices of dissent. Wilson in 1916 dressed up his presidential election campaign with the slogan "He Kept Us Out of War," but his actions gave the lie to his words. Not one American in ten thousand wished to intervene in a quarrel between the British and German monarchies; even the most feeble of presidents could have kept America out of the war, but only "a president of uncommon ability, boldness and flaunting ambition [again the phrase is Walter Karp's] could possibly have gotten us into it." A British diplomat in Washington explained the difficulty in a letter to his superiors in London: "The great bulk of the Americans simply do not believe that the present conflict, whatever its upshot, touches their national security or endangers their power to hold fast to their own ideals of politics, society and ethics." Robert Bacon, a U.S. State Department functionary writing to a friend in England, reduced the problem to one of elementary arithmetic. "In America," he wrote, "there are 50,000 people who understand the necessity of the United States entering the war immediately on your side. But there are 100 million Americans who have not even thought of it. Our task is to see that the figures are reversed." The fifty thousand loyalists were to be found in New York financial circles, among fashionable parsons, impressionable society hostesses, and Anglophile literary gentlemen.

As exclusive as the claque of neoconservative think-tank intellectuals whispering into the ears of the Bush administration, the little crowd of admirers applauding Wilson's grand strategy did so with similar reference to fortuitous circumstance, false rumor, and an abundant store of bad faith. The sinking in February 1898 of the American battleship USS *Maine* in Havana Bay, and of the British liner *Lusitania* off the coast of Ireland in May 1915, provided the early promoters of American empire with *casus belli* like the one presented to the Bush administration by the destruction of the World Trade towers in September 2001. Spain's fifth-rate colonial power in Cuba was depicted by the McKinley administration as "the most wicked despotism there is today on this earth"; Germany in the summer of 1915 was said to be capable of landing, in a matter of sixteen days, 387,000 troops on the coast of New Jersey—a feat of arms equaled by Saddam's supposed ability to fire weapons of mass destruction within a matter of forty-five minutes; McKinley's deliberately subverting all Spanish efforts at negotiation and Wilson's repeatedly refusing a possible peace treaty with Germany were comparable to the Bush administration's overriding of the UN Security Council's motion for further weapons inspections in Iraq; both the McKinley and the Wilson administrations were served by a warmongering press ascribing atrocities to Spanish viceroys (Cuban peasants fed to sharks) and to German generals (Belgian nuns roasted over burning coals), as promptly on cue as Fox News charged Saddam Hussein with the slaughter of Iraqi infants; any and all opponents of the war in Europe were castigated as "poltroons" and "mollycoddles" in the same hysterical tones of voice as the editorials in the *Weekly Standard* berating

Barbra Streisand for her leftist politics or Harvard University for its retreat from the wisdom of William James.

If *The Politics of War* revises the conventional portrait of American foreign policy as a lesson in Christian goodwill, it also suggests that Wilson pursued a course to war in Europe because he wished to play the part of a great statesman settling upon the tumult of nations a peace worthy of comparison to an act of God. Senator Robert La Follette (R.-Wis.) objected to the project on the grounds that Wilson was "a man of high ideals but no principle . . . for him the rhetoric of the thing is the thing itself," and without an American army in Europe so vain a man as Wilson couldn't strike as handsome a pose as the one arranged for President Bush in May 2003 on the flight deck of the USS *Abraham Lincoln*. If the setting-up of Wilson's photo op required the deaths of one hundred thousand American soldiers in the mud of France, the sacrifice could be written off to America's privilege "to spend her blood and her might for the principles that gave her birth."*

Against the will and better judgment of 90 percent of the American people, the United States entered World War I in April 1917. Two months later, in an atmosphere as clouded by militant paranoia as the mind of Attorney General Ash-

---

*The falsity of Wilson's pose as a man of elevated principle and noble character moved Karp to savage mockery, and a single sentence can be taken as indicative of both the sense of his argument and the strength of his prose: "The decisive trait of Wilson's political character was vainglory: a hunger for glory so exclu-

croft, Congress passed the Espionage Act, which defined as criminal any word or action judged to be interfering with what was arbitrarily interpreted as "the national defense." The distributions of punishment were harsh and swift. The Justice Department deputized private citizens to question and hold for arrest any of their neighbors suspected of being slow to swear allegiance to the nearest flag, and by August 1917, Attorney General Thomas Gregory boasted that he had several hundred thousand people working for him as spies.*

Eugene V. Debs, the leader of the American Socialist Party, who had received one million votes in the 1912 presidential election, made the mistake of delivering a speech at Canton, Ohio, on June 16, 1918, in which he described the act as un-constitutional in both character and intent. He was promptly arrested and sentenced to ten years in prison. Rose Pastor

---

sively self-regarding, so indifferent to the concerns of others, that it would lead him to betray in turn the national movement for reform, the great body of the American people, the fundamental liberties of the American Republic, and in the end the hopes of a war-torn world."

Benito Mussolini found in Wilson's handling of the American war effort his reason to abandon the socialist left and embrace the truth of fascism. On September 28, 1917, in his newspaper, *Il Popolo d'Italia,* Mussolini wrote approvingly of Wilson's high-minded lies. "In matters pertaining to the war," he said, "Wilson applies systems of such anti-liberalism that in Italy they would never occur even to the most ferocious reactionaries."

*When twelve hundred mine workers declared a strike in Bisbee, Arizona, in July 1917, they were rounded up by a posse of armed vigilantes, forced into railroad freight cars, shipped to New Mexico, and abandoned in a desert.

Stokes, the editor of the socialist *Jewish Daily News,* informed the Women's Dining Club of Kansas City that "no government which is for the profiteers can also be for the people, and I am for the people while the government is for the profiteers." She, too, was sentenced to ten years in prison. So was a Hollywood film producer who exhibited a motion picture, *The Spirit of '76,* grounded on the plotlines of the American Revolution. The Redcoats appeared in what the government enforcers regarded as an unfavorable light, the film therefore "criminally calculated to make us a little bit slack in our loyalty to Great Britain in this great catastrophe." The post office excluded from the mails the August issue of *The Masses,* a monthly journal of irreverent opinion that routinely published articles written by Sherwood Anderson, Max Eastman, John Reed, and Carl Sandburg. The post office found fault with a poem praising Emma Goldman and a cartoon depicting the figure of a naked youth stuffed into the mouth of a cannon. When the journal sought injunction from the ruling, the case moved into a U.S. district court where the arguments were heard before Judge Learned Hand. The judge well understood the consequences of his failure to agree with Postmaster General Albert S. Burleson. Under consideration that year for promotion to the Court of Appeals, Hand wrote a letter to his wife saying that if he reached the impolitic decision, "then, whoop-la, your little man is in the mud." He nevertheless found in favor of *The Masses,* and the government was not slow to bring the mud. The appellate court promptly reversed the decision; Hand was passed over for promotion; seven of the journal's staff members were indicted for conspiring to violate the Espionage Act; circulation dropped; and by the end of 1917, *The Masses* was out of business.

Augmented in May 1918 by the Sedition Act, which imposed fines and prison terms on anyone disposed to "utter, print, write or publish any disloyal, profane, scurrilous or abusive language about the form of government in the United States," the Espionage Act served as pretext, from the first to the last day of America's participation in the Great War, for a concerted onslaught against the freedom of speech, the right of assembly, the protection against unreasonable search and seizure, and the right to a fair trial. Nothing was to be said or read in America that cast doubt on the nobility of Wilson's goals, on the sublimity of his motives or the efficacy of his statecraft. Frederick Howe, a lawyer allied with Wilson as both a friend and a political adviser, failed to dissuade the president from his pursuit of perfect agreement, and he came away from the conversation thinking that Wilson "was eager for the punishment of men who differed from him, and that there was something vindictive in his eyes as he spoke."*

The signing of the Armistice in November 1918 didn't rescind the Wilson administration's fiat declaring dissent a mark of disloyalty and disloyalty a crime. In place of the German kaiser, the Justice Department substituted the Bolshevik Revolution (the "Hun" traded for the "Red") and set briskly

---

*Again Walter Karp, in *The Politics of War:* "Americans under Lincoln enjoyed every liberty that could possibly be spared; in a war safely fought 3,000 miles from our own shores, Americans under Wilson lost every liberty they could possibly be deprived of."

about the task of arresting individuals with funny-sounding Slavic names. On May 1, 1919, several homemade bombs arrived in the mail for prominent government officials in Washington, among them A. Mitchell Palmer, the newly appointed attorney general; taken together with the continuing labor unrest in Pennsylvania and Ohio and a series of race riots disturbing the peace of West Virginia and Alabama, the terrorist bomb-o-grams resulted in that year's "Red Scare." Palmer published a popular and bestselling essay in which he decried "tongues of revolutionary heat licking the altars of the churches, leaping into the belfry of the school bell, crawling into the sacred corner of American homes, seeking to replace marriage vows with libertine laws, burning up the foundations of society." The United States at the time harbored a cadre of no more than seventy thousand professed Communists (0.067 percent of a population of 104.5 million), but they furnished an explanation for all of the country's unhappiness, and by 1920 Palmer's deputy, the young but already paranoid J. Edgar Hoover, had compiled dossiers on two million American citizens suspected of an illicit relationship with the ideas of Karl Marx. Without warrants or any findings of fact, the Justice Department during the same thirteen months arrested or deported ten thousand alien residents (among them Emma Goldman) rumored to have said something critical of the United States. When the constitutional question was placed before the Supreme Court, Justice Oliver Wendell Holmes wrote the majority opinion, approving the arrests on the grounds that the government may suspend the First Amendment when the exercise of free speech constitutes what it judges to be "a clear and present danger." The ruling affirmed the sentencing of a Connecticut haber-dasher to six months in jail for having said that Lenin was smart, also the twenty-year prison sentence given a rancher in Montana for refusing to kiss the flag.

The return in the 1920s to President Warren Harding's promised state of "normalcy" brought with it rising stock market prices, the joys of jazz and women in short skirts, F. Scott Fitzgerald's vision of a Dionysian future, Charles Lindbergh's flight to Paris, and Babe Ruth's supremacy in Yankee Stadium. The muckraking magazines once renowned for their discovery of corruption on Wall Street printed hymns of praise to the glories of big business. Although the vast majority of the American people weren't invited to the party of the Roaring Twenties (the farmers were desperate, and there were no raccoon coats for the urban poor), the news media deleted the ugliness of political dissent from their portraits of America, the land of milk and honey. In an essay written for *Harper's Magazine* in 1927, the historian Will Durant remarked on what he called "this humorless anomaly":

> Partly it is a corollary of our wealth: the same riches that make us timidly conservative in politics make us bravely liberal in morals; it is as difficult to be ascetic with full pockets as it is, with full pockets to be a revolutionist. . . .
>
> Partly the situation issues from a contradiction in our

hearts: it is the same soul that hungers for the license of liberty and the security of order; the same mind that hovers, in its fluctuating strength and fear, between pride in its freedom and admiration for the police. There are moments when we are anarchists, and moments when we are Prussians. In America above all—in this land of the brave and this home of the free—we are a little fearful of liberty. Our forefathers were free in politics, and stoically stern in morals; they respected the Decalogue, and defied the State. But we deify the State, and riddle the Decalogue; we are Epicureans in morals, but we submit to all but one of a hundred thousand laws; we are slaves in politics, and free only in our cups.

The sorrows of the Great Depression forced the renewal of an interest both in anarchists and in the revolutionary adjustments of Franklin Roosevelt's New Deal. In the center ring of American politics, the president established a program of social reform that guaranteed payment of a minimum wage and a government pension; in the more volatile sectors of principled opinion, a generation of American intellectuals (screenwriters and newspaper editors as well as novelists and poets) toyed with the romance of communism. Literary reputation and academic tenure accrued to the accounts of enlightened authors who discovered in Stalin the savior of an oppressed people. John Steinbeck's *The Grapes of Wrath* appeared in 1939, Ernest Hemingway's *For Whom the Bell Tolls* in 1940, and in the cafés of Greenwich Village many of the young *soi-disant* revolutionaries, later to become staunch apologists for Reaganism (among them James Burnham and Irving Kristol), professed their faith in Leon Trotsky. Among the proprietors of small literary journals, so giddy was the enthusiasm for the color red that the authorities in Washington were reawakened to their old fear of bearded Slavs docking in New York Harbor with copies of V. I. Lenin's "What Is to Be Done?" and suitcases stuffed with nitroglycerin. Congress in 1938 set up the House Un-American Activities Committee to investigate persons believed capable of unpatriotic thoughts or deeds; the Alien Registration Act of 1940 required all foreign residents of the United States over the age of fourteen to file a summation of their personal and occupational status as well as full disclosure of their political beliefs. Within four months the government registered nearly five million names.*

The Communist menace disappeared from the American theaters of intellectual operation for the duration of World War II. Joined as allies against the common enemy of Nazi Germany, the Soviet Union and the United States declared

---

*During the first months after the attack on Pearl Harbor, the federal government incarcerated seventy thousand American citizens for no reason other than their Japanese ancestry. Explaining the maneuver to a congressional committee, Lieutenant General John DeWitt anticipated the Bush administration's reasons for rounding up Muslims after the attacks on New York and Washington. "A Jap's a Jap," the general said. "It makes no difference whether he is an American citizen or not."

themselves comrades-in-arms and the best of friends. Franklin Roosevelt and Winston Churchill sat down with *Time* magazine's "good old Uncle Joe Stalin" at Yalta in February 1945 to divide the spoils of the soon-to-arrive victory in Europe, and when forward elements of the Russian army encountered forward elements of the American army on German soil in April 1945, the soldiers marked the occasion with rousing songs and clumsy dances. The moment of good feeling didn't last through Christmas. Forgetful of the agreement reached at Yalta, the Soviet armies placed the countries of Eastern Europe behind what Churchill in the spring of 1946 declared to be an "Iron Curtain," and by 1947 the Truman administration had drawn up the blueprint of the military and industrial architecture of the cold war.

The government's nervousness was not unreasonable. Europe in the late 1940s looked like a postcard from the Russian Revolution, and although the Allies had won the war against Hitler in the name of democratic freedom and Western civilization, they appeared to be losing the peace to Stalin and the theories of totalitarian paradise. The Vienna Woods had been burned for fuel, and across the whole of France, Germany, the Low Countries, and the Baltic states, thirteen million refugees, reduced to near starvation and dying in the bitter cold, wandered the streets of ruined cities, foraging for rats and sleeping in holes. The abundant signs of misery gave credence to the voices crying up the hope of Communist salvation. In Paris as in Rome, the rumors of leftist coups d'état drifted noisily through the cafés; Soviet youth groups were on the march in Munich and Milan, labor unions up in arms in Barcelona and Marseilles, university professors handing out Marxist leaflets on the boulevards of Brussels, Lisbon, and Cologne. Against the backdrop of trouble elsewhere in the world (nationalist uprisings in the colonies of imperial Britain, China under the dominion of Mao Tsetung, President Wilson's theory of political self-determination making inroads across the African continent), the Russian blockade of Berlin in 1948, followed in 1949 by the test-firing of the Soviet atomic bomb, prompted the Truman administration to build what was known to the tabloid press as Fortress America. The Communists were obviously telling lies, and the friends of free expression understood that one didn't sally forth onto the field of Armageddon armed only with the simple truth. George F. Kennan advanced the "messianic concept" of "the necessary lie," which embraced the virtues of plausible deniability, the vocabularies of misleading statement, the manufacture of ideological consent. He set forth the theory of American omnipotence in a memorandum circulated within the State Department during the winter of 1948:

We have about 50% of the world's wealth, but only 6.3% of its population . . . in this situation, we cannot fail to be the object of envy and resentment. Our real task in the coming period is to devise a pattern of relationships which will permit us to maintain this position of disparity without positive detriment to our national security. To do so, we will have to dispense with all sentimentality and daydreaming.*

Dean Acheson, who later became Truman's secretary of state, already had understood that if the United States wished to do as it pleased in the world, it would be necessary to come up with a slogan that could serve as both a reason and an explanation for high-handed, unilateral decisions. Knowing that the American people might balk at the prospect of the cold war if they thought the strategy open to discussion, Acheson in 1947 explained to his associates in Georgetown that the country's foreign policy must be presented as "non-partisan," that any and all political argument "stops at the water's edge."

"If we can make them believe that," Acheson said, "we're off to the races."

The stopping of all political argument at the water's edge was made easier by raising the fear of communism to the power of near hysteria. Truman in 1947 issued Executive Or-

---

*The preferred "patterns of relationship" presupposed an American realpolitik strongly turned away from what Kennan regarded as "unreal objectives such as human rights, the raising of living standards and democratization." The young Winston Churchill, a member of the Liberal opposition in the British Parliament in 1904, ascribed a similar pattern of relationship to the Tory government, then charged with the supervision of an empire on which the sun never set. "A party of great vested interests," Churchill said, "banded together in a formidable confederation, corruption at home, aggression to cover it up abroad . . . sentiment by the bucketful, patriotism by the imperial pint, the open hand at the public exchequer, the open door at the public house, dear food for the millions, cheap labor for the millionaire." The description matches the profile of our own Bush administration.

der 9835 (aka "the Loyalty Oath"), requiring the Justice Department to winnow from the ranks of Washington's officialdom any "disloyal persons" consorting with, or in any way connected to, organizations deemed "totalitarian, fascist, Communist or subversive." That same year the House Un-American Activities Committee undertook its investigation of the motion picture industry, which resulted in the sending of ten screenwriters to prison (among them Ring Lardner Jr. and Dalton Trumbo) and the composition of the Hollywood Blacklist, which marked 320 individuals as unfit to work in front of a camera or behind a scene.* In 1948 in New York City, eleven American citizens who also happened to be members of the Communist Party were brought to trial for the crime of political heresy. Accused of advocating the principles of Marxist-Leninism, they were convicted of intent to overthrow the United States and sent to prison with the approval of the Supreme Court.

By 1950 the United States was at war in Korea—33,000 American soldiers recruited to die in a campaign they never had a chance to win—and back home in Kansas and Indiana, angry and frightened voices were asking how and why the world could have gone so wrong. Senator Joseph McCarthy of Wisconsin

---

*Among those blacklisted—Leonard Bernstein, Charlie Chaplin, Aaron Copland, John Garfield, Dashiell Hammett, Lillian Hellman, Burl Ives, Arthur Miller, Clifford Odets, Dorothy Parker, Paul Robeson, Pete Seeger, Louis Untermeyer, Orson Welles, and Richard Wright.

soon discovered 225 traitors lurking in the closets of government ("I have here in my hand a list"), and the country was off, if not to the races, at least on a hunt similar to the one conducted in Salem, Massachusetts, in 1692 by Puritan clergymen searching the town for as many witches as could be found guilty of conspiring with Satan. Like the colonial magistrates quick to award the judgment of death, the senator from Wisconsin accepted rumors as evidence and accused anybody and everybody who could be placed at the scene of a subversive thought. Both sets of interrogation relied on the testimony of fear.

Between 1947 and 1954 no fewer than 6.6 million Americans fell into the nets of government investigations strung together with illegal wiretaps, false testimony, and synthetic evidence. While McCarthy's Senate permanent subcommittee on investigations set about the search for fellow travelers believed to be "soft on Communism" (among them George Marshall and William Benton, the publisher of the *Encyclopaedia Britannica*), the State Department purged from its libraries in foreign cities any and all books suspected of treason (thirty thousand volumes under forty titles, among them *The Selected Works of Thomas Jefferson*). Hollywood produced a parade of patriotic movies (fifty of them in six years) along the lines of *I Married a Communist* and *I Was a Communist for the FBI*. The large-circulation magazines contributed cautionary tales ("How Communists Get That Way," "Communists Are After Your Child"), and Mickey Spillane, the most popular author of the day, sold three million copies of *One Lonely*

Night, a novel anticipating the oeuvre of Tom Clancy, in which the hero, Mike Hammer, comes to the rescue of America the Good, America the Fair—for example, "I killed more people tonight than I have fingers on my hands. I shot them in cold blood and enjoyed every minute of it . . . they were Commies, Red sons-of-bitches who should have died long ago."

The *New York Times* in 1956 took the precaution of publishing an editorial tantamount to a loyalty oath: "We would not knowingly employ a Communist Party member in the news or editorial department . . . because we would not trust his ability to report the news objectively or to comment on it honestly." And in Wheeling, West Virginia, the city manager, who discovered fifty vending machines in his city dispensing sticks of chewing gum sometimes accompanied by a pasteboard trinket inscribed with a hammer and sickle and the words "USSR, pop. 211,000,000, capital Moscow," responded, alertly and at once, to the threat of Communist infiltration. "That's a terrible thing to expose the children of this city to," he said. "I have demanded a complete investigation. Names of store owners to whom the machines were licensed have been turned over to the FBI."*

---

*The history of the McCarthy era speaks not only to the malevolence of the investigations but also to the paranoia that often verges into the theater of the absurd. Thus the questioning of a Brooklyn Navy Yard worker identified only as M:

Loyalty Board Member: "What book clubs do you subscribe to?"
M: "The Book Find Club."
LBM: "Does Feuchtwanger write for them? Does Dreiser contribute? Some

Whether located in the universities, the newspapers, or the New York literary arena, the vast majority of the country's prominent intellectuals (novelists as well as playwrights and historians) submitted in silence to the intolerant temper of the times. Arthur Miller and Henry Steele Commager proved themselves exceptions to the rule of cowardice; so did Archibald MacLeish, who, in 1949 in "The Conquest of America," drew the moral from the lesson that despotism teaches to democracy:

> Never in the history of the world was one people as completely dominated, intellectually and morally, by another as the people of the United States by the people of Russia in the four years from 1946 through 1949. American foreign policy was a mirror image of Russian foreign policy; whatever the Russians did, we did in reverse. American domestic politics were conducted under a kind of upside-down Russian veto; no man could be elected to public office unless he was on record as detesting the Russians, and no proposal could be enacted, from a peace plan at one end to a military budget at the other, unless it could be demonstrated that the Russians wouldn't like it. American political controversy was controversy sung to the Russian tune. . . . All this took place not in a time of national weakness or decay but precisely at the moment when the United States,

---

of their writers adhere to the Communist Party line, did you know that? They weave doctrine into a story."

M: "I ain't that much of a genius. I read the words, not the weaving."

having engineered a tremendous triumph and fought its way to a brilliant victory in the greatest of all wars, had reached the highest point of world power ever achieved by a single state.

The totalitarian model served the parties of great vested interest in Washington intent on replacing the antiquated American Republic, modest in ambition and democratic in spirit, with what President Dwight David Eisenhower foresaw as the eventual colossus of a "military-industrial complex," the likes of which the world had never seen—weapons of every conceivable caliber and size, a vast armada of naval vessels afloat on eight seas and seven oceans, guidance systems as infallible as the pope, tracking devices blessed with the judgment of a recording angel. Fattened on the seed of open-handed military spending ($17 trillion since 1950) and grazing on the pastures of easy credit and certain profit, the divine arsenal now encompasses 798 military installations in at least forty countries. The rich displays of armament bear comparison with religious statuary. No matter what the specific function of the weapons, as attack submarines or high-altitude gun platforms, they stand as symbols representative of the divinity (absolute, unfathomable, unseen but always present) implicit in the cloud of nuclear unknowing. To the blessed work of making weapons we assign our finest intellect and the largest share of our treasure, and in the magnificence of an aircraft carrier or a cruise missile we find the moral and aesthetic equivalent of the Sistine ceiling and Chartres Cathedral. In the presence of the sacred, the servants of American empire define as blasphemy the noise and scratching of dissent.

During the 1960s as many as one hundred government agencies (state, federal, and municipal) set up clandestine surveillance of citizens objecting to the Vietnam War, demonstrating on behalf of the civil rights movement, talking too loudly in favor of women's rights. The Department of Defense conducted warrantless searches of college dormitories in order to provide President Lyndon Johnson with a report entitled *Restless Youth;* the Secret Service compiled a list of persons to be rounded up in the event of a "national emergency." The CIA's numerous investigations were assembled under the code name CHAOS, those conducted by the FBI under the acronym COINTELPRO. Dredging more or less the same pool of suspects for the same kind of opinions, temporarily out of uniform, the two armies of inspectors general combined over a period of twenty years to amass files on several million of their fellow Americans, to open and photograph five hundred thousand pieces of first-class mail, to infiltrate innumerable political and quasi-political organizations, and to jail, entrap, intimidate, or misinform several hundred thousand people against whom, when occasion arose, they also deployed the techniques of blackmail, false arrest, and timely assassination.* In 1976, subsequent to the discov-

---

*Among those under investigation—Students for a Democratic Society, the Lawyers Guild, Columbia University, the Gay-Lesbian Alliance, Vietnam Veterans Against the War, Princeton University, Tom Hayden, Dave Dellinger, Jane

ery of the Nixon administration's complicity in the Watergate burglaries, a congressional committee under the chairmanship of Senator Frank Church (D.-Idaho) published a report entitled *Intelligence Activities and the Rights of Americans*. The summary finding didn't mince its words:

> Too many people have been spied upon by too many government agencies and too much information has been collected. The government has often undertaken the secret surveillance of citizens on the basis of their political beliefs, even when those beliefs pose no threat of violence or illegal acts on behalf of a hostile foreign power. . . . Investigations have been based upon vague standards whose breadth made excessive collection inevitable. Unsavory and vicious tactics have been employed—including anonymous attempts to break up marriages, disrupt meetings, ostracize persons from their professions, and provoke target groups into rivalries that might result in deaths. Intelligence agencies have served the political and personal objectives of presidents and other high officials . . . government officials—including those whose principal duty is to enforce the law—have violated or ignored the law over long periods of time and have advocated and defended their right to break the law.

Fonda, John Lennon, Jean Seberg; black nationalist hate groups, the Black Panthers, Martin Luther King Jr., Bobby Seale, Eldridge Cleaver, Fred Hampton, H. Rap Brown, Elijah Muhammad, Huey Newton, Malcolm X.

Any corrections of behavior that the government might have thought to undertake during the years of relative good feeling associated with both the Reagan and Clinton administrations went missing in the smoke on the morning of September 11, 2001. The enhanced powers of law enforcement embedded in the PATRIOT and Homeland Security Acts aspire to a new and improved system of bureaucratic control that joins the paranoid systems of thought engendered by the cold war with the surveillance techniques made possible by the miracles of our digitally enhanced telecommunications technology. The CIA might not know where to find Osama bin Laden; the FBI might lose track of two murderous Al Qaeda operatives who listed their address in the San Diego phone book while learning how to fly a plane into the World Trade Center; but when it comes to the tactical deployment of a flowchart, the mobilization of new investigative guidelines, or the strategic reenforcement of a press statement, our field commanders in Washington show themselves the equals of Napoleon.

The meaning of the words tends to get lost in the barrage of patriotic slogan that obscures the landscapes of defeat, but the confusion proved useful to the news conference on May 30, 2002, at which the Justice Department announced, for the third time in almost as many months, yet another reorganization of the FBI. Attorney General John Ashcroft executed the maneuver with his customary audacity, supporting it with so many deft flanking movements (among them the concealment of his plan from Congress) that it wasn't easy to follow the line of his advance or to know who he thought was the enemy. The fact sheet distributed by the federal publicity agents (*Crafting an Overall Blueprint for Change, Reshaping the FBI's Priorities*) came with a number of attachments (*The Use of Confidential Informants, Terrorism Enterprise Investigations, General Crimes, Undercover Operations*), which in every instance served either as an excuse for incompetence or as a claim to extrajudicial privilege.

The attorney general didn't name any names or lay the blame at the feet of godless politicians, but neither did he try to hide the thought that if the FBI had been allowed to do its job, the twin towers might still be standing watch over the lower reaches of the Hudson River. Unfortunately for America and the American way of life, the bureau for the last thirty years had been crippled by "organizational and operational restrictions," bound up in "unnecessary procedural red tape." Never mind that the restrictions were imposed for good reason when it was discovered, as per the Church Committee's report, that the FBI had been running illegal intelligence operations against as many as two million American citizens suspected of opposing the war in Vietnam or supporting the civil rights movement. What the fact sheet billed as the bold shifting of emphasis "from prosecution to prevention" unbinds Prometheus, removes the hobbles of bureaucratic restraint, and puts an end to the timid and overly literal-minded deference to the language of the Bill of Rights. No longer will the FBI's eleven thousand agents sit feebly in their chairs filling out forms, asking permission to look out the window, waiting to "sift through the rubble following a terrorist attack"; they will "intervene early and investigate aggressively where information exists suggesting the possibility of terrorism."

The *Terrorism Enterprise Investigations* guidelines grant the FBI license to commit crimes when and if the circumstances warrant an especially strong defense of the public safety and the common good. The more serious felonies, of course, still require authorization from FBI headquarters in Washington or the special agents in charge of a regional office, but such authorization is not to be unreasonably withheld (not when innocent American lives are at stake), and if time doesn't allow for a written confirmation, the money laundering, the giving and taking of bribes, the winking at murder, the search, seizure, and entrapment of likely suspects can go forward on a word whispered into a secure telephone or an unmarked car.

Among the new FBI special units put in place since September 11, the fact sheet happily listed "the Financial Review Group, the Document Exploitation Group, and E-mail Exploitation Group . . . the Telephone Applications Group, as well as the Threat, Warning, Analysis and Dissemination Groups." Briskly efficient and blandly abstract, the terminology favors the classification of civil rights as nuisances that get in the way of law enforcement officers rummaging through bank records and lingerie drawers in order to protect the American people from the swarm of terrorists in their midst. Ashcroft spoke to the need for a new understanding of the word "protection" by explaining, once again, that the onerous regulations under which the FBI had been operating for the last thirty years "mistakenly combined timeless objectives—the enforcement of the law and respect for civil rights and liberties—with outdated means."*

As modified by the context and subject to the circumstances, the phrase "outdated means" can be taken to refer to any paragraph in every article of the Constitution. Which is both good to know and important to bear in mind, because a modern war against terrorism cannot be fought with an old scrap of parchment and obsolete notions of freedom. Let too many freedoms wander around loose in the streets, and who knows when somebody will turn up with a bread knife or a bomb? Better to remember the lesson learned in the Vietnam War, which proved that the best way to save the village was to destroy it. So also now, in another time of trouble, the American people can best preserve their liberties by sending them to a taxidermist or donating them to a museum.†

---

*When dealing with government police officials, the loosening of restraints is seldom a good idea. Louis Freeh, director of the FBI during the Clinton administration, put the matter as plainly as it can be put in June 1997, in testimony before the House Judiciary Committee's subcommittee on crime. "We are," he said, "the most dangerous agency in the country if we are not scrutinized carefully."

†On Christmas Eve 2003, the FBI issued a bulletin advising eighteen thousand of the country's law enforcement agencies to watch out for people carrying almanacs. Almanacs, said the FBI, can be used by terrorists "to assist with target selection and pre-operational planning." Because almanacs contain information, often accompanied by photographs and maps, about waterways, bridges, dams, reservoirs, tunnels, buildings, and roads, anyone carrying such a thing might be a terrorist or a friend of a terrorist. It was suggested that police officers approach with caution all almanacs "annotated in suspicious ways."

In the meantime, as true Americans waiting for further instructions, they can serve their country by playing the part of stool pigeons. The fact sheet put out a casting call for informants of every known description—for neighborhood gossips and public scolds as well as for professional criminals and amateur conspiracy theorists. Improving on the methods available to Attorney General Gregory in 1917, the supplemental guideline noted both a Web site and a toll-free telephone number, together with the heartening news that in the months of April and May the FBI had received 225,000 tips by e-mail, and 180,000 tips over the phone. No power point indicated the number of agents assigned to the task of sorting out the false rumors from the groundless suspicions and the vengeful slanders; nor did the fact sheet refer to the number of agents currently listening to wiretaps and peering at the film footage captured by the several million surveillance cameras now stationed at all points on the American compass. Constant supervision on so vast a scale must add to the burden of "unnecessary procedural red tape," which presented a contradiction again suggesting that Ashcroft's reorganization of the FBI serves a purpose other than the one announced at press conferences. A well-ordered police state rests on the cornerstone of a cowed citizenry, and how better to promote a decent respect for authority than by encouraging people to imagine themselves wearing a sheriff's badge, a well-tailored uniform, and a pair of polished boots?

In New York these days nobody moves from dawn to dusk without making as many as thirty or forty cameo appearances on the reality TV programs that are continuously being filmed in the city's stores, office and apartment buildings, restaurants, airports, jails, sports stadiums, and full-service limousines. In the spring of 2002, without public knowledge or city council approval, the police department in Washington installed a network of video cameras throughout the District of Columbia, on lampposts and street corners, in subway stations and public schools, tracking tourists and delivery trucks as well as office clerks and visiting heads of state. The federal Department of Transportation meanwhile proposed to classify all commercial airline passengers as potential terrorists and therefore subject—simply by buying a ticket from one destination to any other—to background investigations that otherwise might require a court order.

The variants on the gag rule now add up to so large a number that although I've yet to see a comprehensive list, I can read the handwriting on the government wall. Money is beautiful and must be sheltered from the tax authorities and the rain; mere human beings, by nature unstable and rebellious, must be placed under strict surveillance and control. Heavy concentrations of large capital remain at liberty to do as they please—to poison rivers, cut down forests, charge cruel rates of interest, experiment with lethal chemicals, deny medical care, eliminate species, repudiate debts, live handsomely beyond their income. Unincorporated individuals wait for instructions about where and when they can sing or talk or smoke or dance. If not going off to prison for the possession of a single joint of marijuana, they submit to the censorship of their careless and ill-kempt speech—corporations dismiss employees for passing salacious e-mail; the city of San Diego forbids the use of the word "minority" on any municipal piece of paper, no more than fifty people may assemble on the steps of New York's City Hall. The FBI searches large-scale street demonstrations for "anarchists" and "extremist elements," arrests at random any participant deemed eligible for a lesson in obedience.* When President Bush travels around the country to praise the freedoms for which America presumably is famous, the Secret Service sends advance scouts to set up "free-speech areas" for citizens wishing to voice objections or display signs critical of the president's policies. Quarantined behind chain-link fences at a discreet distance from the presidential motorcade (preferably out of earshot and far enough away to avoid notice on the evening news), the protesters remain free to shout at one another.

President Bush likes to tell his military and civilian audiences that, as Americans, "we refuse to live in fear," and of all lies told by the government's faith healers and gun salesmen, I know of none so cowardly. Where else does the Bush administration ask the American people to live except in fear? On what other grounds does it justify its destruction of the nation's civil liberties? Ever since the September 11 at-

---

*The point being to discourage further experiments with the theory of free speech and make clear the penalty for poor deportment. An arrest record complicates the career plans for young and maybe upwardly mobile students obliged to meet the character requirements for admission to a prestigious bank or law firm. Step out of line, my son, and you can say good-bye to the good-hands people at Allstate.

tacks on New York and Washington, no week has passed in which the government has failed to issue warnings of a sequel. Sometimes it's the director of the FBI, sometimes the attorney general or an unnamed source in the CIA or the Department of Homeland Security, but always it's the same message: Suspect your neighbor and watch the sky, buy duct tape, avoid the Washington Monument, hide the children. Let too many citizens begin to ask impertinent questions about the shambles of the federal budget or the disappearance of a forest in Montana, and the government sends another law-enforcement officer to a microphone with a story about a missing tube of plutonium or a newly discovered nerve gas.

As unrelenting as the Justice Department in its search for the roots of all evil, the Defense Department in early 2002 established an Information Awareness Office that took for its emblem the all-seeing eye of God and recruited a synod of high-speed computers capable of sifting through "ultra-large" data warehouses stocked with every electronic proof of human movement in the wilderness of cyberspace—bank, medical, and divorce records; credit card transactions; e-mails (interoffice and extraterritorial); college transcripts; surveillance photographs (from cameras in hospitals and shopping malls as well as from those in airports and hotel bars); driver's licenses and passport applications; bookstore purchases; Web site visits; and traffic violations. Connect all the names and places to all the dates and times, and once the systems become fully operational, in four years or maybe ten, the protectors of the public health and safety hope to reach beyond "truth maintenance" and "biologically in-spired algorithms for agent control" to the construction of "FuturMap"—that is, a set of indices programmed into the fiber-optic equivalent of a crystal ball that modifies "market-based techniques for avoiding surprise" in such a way that next week's nuclear explosion can be seen as clearly as last week's pornographic movie.*

The country clearly confronts unscrupulous enemies who mean to do us no small harm, but if I can't quarrel with the government's improvement of the means with which to per-form an urgent and difficult task, neither do I put much faith in its declarations of democratic principle and intent. Not-withstanding its habitual incompetence, the government doesn't lightly relinquish the spoils of power seized under the pretexts of apocalypse. What the government grasps, the government seeks to keep and hold, and too many of its re-formulated purposes fit too neatly with the Bush administra-tion's wish to set itself above the law. Often when watching the official spokespeople address a television audience, I'm reminded of corporate lawyers talking to a crowd of recently bankrupted shareholders, and usually I'm left with the im-pression that they would like to put the entire country be-hind a one-way mirror that allows the government to see the people but prevents the people from seeing it.

And for what? To exact vengeance on a resentful com-

---

*The effort was temporarily suspended when reports of the IAO's existence es-caped into the mainstream press in November 2002.

pany of threadbare assassins, many of them barefoot and not yet twenty, who can find no other way out of the alleys of their despair except with the exit visa of a suicide bomb? As a consequence of civilization's war on terror, America gains immediate access to an unlimited fund of unspecific rage. In return for so poor a victory, the Bush administration asks the American people to deny their dearest principles, to repudiate their civil liberties and repent of the habits of freedom. The deal is as shabby as the president's lying photo ops. For the sake of a vindictive policeman's dream of a tranquil suburb, the country stands to lose the constitutional right to its own name.

THREE

Mute Button

Without censorship, things can get terribly confused in the public mind.

—GENERAL WILLIAM C. WESTMORELAND

Because the Bush administration takes so little trouble to disguise its contempt for the commonwealth on which it feeds, I often come across people who ask why the national news media make so small a noise of objection and complaint. Where are the voices of conscience, and why no "vigorous dissent" on the part of the fair and free press designated to uphold the Constitution against the ambition of its enemies? In parking lots and hotel bars, at dinner tables in uptown restaurants and downtown lofts, the questions reflect a general concern for the sturdiness of the First Amendment as well as the preferences for a specific political point of view. Sometimes the questioners mention the conservative bias embedded in the walls of Fox News, less often the liberal bias in the drinking water at the *New York Times;* sometimes they refer to the "blithering stupidity" of a particular newspaper columnist or television talk-show host (Paul Krugman is as often and as angrily denounced as Rush Limbaugh and Bill O'Reilly); nearly always they expect the media to deliver not only sensational crime stories and accurate baseball scores but also, at the cost of one dollar or less, wisdom, compassion, and the truth.

It's no good pointing to the alien and seditious titles on any week's bestseller list, to the writings of Noam Chomsky and Howard Zinn, if not also to those of Ann Coulter and Robert Bork. The questions continue and the doubts persist because the obstacles that stand in the way of an honest and genuinely democratic debate consist not only of the prejudices symptomatic of corporate journalism but also of the epistemological biases inherent in both the American school system and the means of electronic communication.

The faults to be found with the news media are as numberless as the pebbles on the beach at Nantucket, but it's a mistake to blame them for the current emptiness of our politics. To do so serves no purpose other than to flatter the media's sense of their own self-importance. Having attended a good many weekend conferences at which various well-placed figures within the peerage of the fourth estate exchanged decorative platitudes while admiring the view of the mountains or the sea, I long ago learned that nothing so alarms the assembled company as the intrusion of a new idea. The nature of the business is commercial, not political, and when the speakers on the dais praise one another as ferocious champions of liberty pacing tirelessly to and fro on the ramparts of freedom, the effect is comic. The ladies and gentlemen seated behind the wineglasses enjoy the patronage of very large, very rich, and very timid corporations (Time Warner, General Electric, the Disney Company), and anybody who rises to prominence in their ranks—as editor, political columnist, publisher, anchorperson, theater critic—learns to think along the accommodating lines of an English butler bringing buttered scones to the Prince of Wales. Contrary to the preferred portrait of the journalist as a relentless seeker after truth, the stock character more nearly representative of the trade would be that of the cupbearer or the cosmetician— a Rosencrantz or Guildenstern forever worrying about the quality and number of his dinner invitations, glad to do the king's bidding, quick to repeat the gossip heard on the palace stairs, a credulous and obliging little friend to all the world.*

Unwilling to take chances with any book, movie, rock song, or situation comedy that doesn't meet the expectations of

---

*The *Wall Street Journal,* probably the most widely read newspaper in the country, heavily favors the conservative side on any and all questions of public policy, and both the *Washington Post* and the *New York Times* fortify their op-ed pages with columnists who strongly defend the established order—William Safire and David Brooks in the *Times;* Charles Krauthammer, George Will, and Richard Harwood in the *Post.* The vast bulk of the nation's radio talk shows (commanding roughly 80 percent of the audience) reflect a reactionary bias, and so do all but one or two of the television talk shows that deal with political topics on PBS, CNN, and CNBC.

On the nation's lecture circuit the voices of reason that attract the biggest crowds and command the highest fees all speak for one or another of the parties of the right. Augmenting the instruments of the nominally secular media, the chorus of religious broadcasts and pamphlets (among them Pat Robertson's *The 700 Club* and the publications under the direction of the Reverend Sun Myung Moon) envelops the country in a stereophonic din of patriotic sound.

what the prospective audiences wish to see and hear, the institutional media preserve the myths the society deems precious, reassuring their patrons that all is well, that the American virtues remain securely in place, that the banks are safe, our doctors competent, our presidents interested in the public welfare, our artists capable of masterpieces, our armies invincible, and our democratic institutions the wonder of an admiring world. Nor does anybody care very much which lies pass for truth. If in one season President Bill Clinton can be promoted and sold as a juvenile delinquent, in another season he can be promoted and sold as an elder statesman—compassionate and wise, the voice of experience and the soul of discretion. Supported by the correct marketing strategy, both editions of the man can be processed into headlines, television chatter, and bestselling biography. The truth is something that Peter Jennings maybe will get around to next summer when he has the time to read *Moby-Dick* or listen to Beethoven's Ninth Symphony.

The media compose the pictures of a preferred reality, and their genius is that of the nervous careerist who serves, simultaneously, two masters—the demos, whom they astound with marvels and fairy tales, and the corporate nobility, whose interests they assiduously promote and defend. The trick is by no means easy. It demands the skill of a juggler or an acrobat, but few of the well-paid adepts admit to talents associated with carnivals and fairs. At the awards banquets and on the annual pilgrimages to the mountains, nobody mentions the media's embarrassing resemblance to a chain of cut-rate department stores. Like all arrivistes jealous of their places in the sun, the high-end columnists and anchor-persons cast themselves in the most flattering available light—as dignified, professional gentlemen and gentlewomen trading at par value with physicians, lawyers, and professors of theology—and they scorn their clumsy and ill-bred relations who don't know when or how to ask a question in the White House Rose Garden. It isn't that the news media object to displays of immoral conduct but rather that they think it their duty to protect the rulers of the state from the howling of the mob, to preserve (for as long as is decently possible) the precious and expensively manufactured images of wisdom and power. They live in mortal fear of being made to look ridiculous.

The education of an American journalist is a courtier's education, and my own introduction to the gallery of mirrors I received as a reporter for the *San Francisco Examiner* and the *New York Herald Tribune,* and then, some years later, as a correspondent for the *Saturday Evening Post* and *Life.* Within a matter of eight or nine months after joining the *Examiner* in the late autumn of 1957, I understood that nothing was to be gained by thinking for oneself. What was true was what somebody important said was true. Only on rare occasions did an editor question the text of an official statement. If the operative paragraphs could be attributed to the seals and stamps of municipal authority—the coroner's office, a police captain, the Department of Parks, the president of I. Magnin, or the chairman of the Bechtel Corporation—the *Examiner* was content to publish nonsense. Itself a bureaucracy, the fourth estate retains a devout faith in bureaucratic paper, and as a reporter loyal to the orthodoxy of "objective journalism" I was bound to accept the press release as the last and best word on the topic. I once asked a sardonic night city editor about the game of let's pretend, and I remember his surprise at the depth of my ignorance. Where had I been for nine months, and what did I think I had been doing? The newspaper business, he said, was a matter of telling stories, some of them more interesting than others, all of them subject to change on short notice. The official announcements could be understood as a series of fantastic tales embodying at best a plausible hope or a remote possibility, soon to be followed— preferably in time for the next edition—by denials, contradictions, further explanations, and more fantastic tales. All the stories were straw with which to make the bricks of the news, and in answer to my remark that journalism wasn't much different from popular fiction, the editor reminded me that most of the information that most people receive in the course of a week or a year—in newsletters, gossip columns, stock market reports, or travel advertisements—sooner or later proves to be a figment of somebody's imagination.

After two years on the *Examiner* I thought the fault was with the paper, not the profession, and I left for New York and the *Herald Tribune,* believing that what was then one of the best newspapers in the country might tolerate the risk of independent thought. The expectation was misplaced. As at the *Examiner,* the habit of subservience was chronic and pervasive. The exchange of misinformation took place in a slightly more elevated sphere—solemnities about the cold war instead of the street crime in Oakland—and the institutional bulletins arrived on more expensive paper under more impressive letterheads—the Ford Foundation and the State Department instead of the Geary Theater or the Golden Gate Bridge Authority—but the rules were the same, and so was the belief that access to privileged information (of knowing what the general public didn't know about politics, art, sin, Europe, Greenwich Village restaurants, and John F. Kennedy's mistresses) conferred the inestimable reward of being in the loop, ahead of the curve, party to the joke.*

None of the senior officials at the paper needed to go to the trouble of explaining the codes of self-censorship. The stories that made page one were the stories that confirmed the resident presuppositions, and an attentive reporter soon learned that the honors of the profession were bestowed on people who could dress up the wisdom of the moment in the costume of a clever or sententious phrase. The man who would be James Reston or Walter Cronkite learned when and where to hold or bite his tongue. If he couldn't do so with unreserved enthusiasm, then he could look forward to being condemned as an eccentric or a curmudgeon—unfit, irre-

---

*Among journalists long accustomed to writing for the institutional press, the fear of coming to one's own conclusions shows up in the pronouns. As managing editor of *Harper's Magazine* in the early 1970s, I once received from a writer employed by *Time* a ten-thousand-word article that until the last paragraph was cast in the omniscient third person. In the final sentence the writer permitted himself the phrase "I think." When he saw the text in second draft, he became so frightened of his lapse into the first-person singular that he changed the phrase to read "millions of people think." The loss of heart assured the rejection of his manuscript.

sponsible, clearly incapable of arranging the language ("missile gap," "new frontier," "third world") into the intellectual scenery deemed fit for the Ford Motor Company or a king.

By 1965 I had become a contract writer for the *Saturday Evening Post,* sent to Washington in April of that year to write about President Lyndon Johnson, and during my first week in the White House press lobby I discovered that the terms of service were the same as those in effect in the San Francisco police precincts and New York's City Hall. The correspondents in attendance did what they were told and took what they were given, and in return for their courtesy and good behavior they were granted the luxury of thinking themselves situated at the center of the universe. They counted among their company thirty or forty permanent representatives from major news organizations who mostly sat around on comfortable couches and chairs, reading the papers, complaining about the ignorance of their editors, deploring the credulity of their readers. Four or five times a day the news was brought to them from the office of George Reedy, the presidential press secretary, who conducted morning and afternoon briefings and arranged for the correspondents to attend one or more of the events listed on the president's daily calendar. The invitations were delivered by one of Reedy's senior assistants, a blond and often sarcastic woman in her middle thirties who wore her hair in an attractive French twist. At random intervals throughout the day she appeared suddenly in the press lobby, raising her voice to the pitch of a public announcement: "Attention, reporters. . . . Attention. I have news. Over here, reporters."

I can still hear the sound of her voice, which was high and clear and peremptory, a voice that brooked no disobedience or delay. All of us rose more or less smartly to our feet and followed wherever she led—to the Rose Garden for a photo opportunity with the prime minister of Ghana, to the theater in the basement to hear a general explain a map, to the South Lawn to watch the president play with his dogs, and during my three-month sojourn in the White House press lobby, I never could escape the impression of a flock of ducks— plump and well-kept ducks, ducks worthy of an emperor's garden—waddling back and forth to the pond on which the emperor's gamekeepers cast the bread crumbs of the news. Servile by need, the media become servile in spirit, willing to trade the capacity to think for the security of being told. Lyndon Johnson referred to his attending press corps as a troupe of "puppets . . . who simply respond to the most powerful strings," a judgment confirmed by Tom Wicker, then the Washington bureau chief for the *New York Times:*

In the end we are still part of the league of gentlemen. The people who run the press—particularly the metropolitan, largely capitalized institutions of the press—are part of it, along with the people who run the government and the major businesses and the big corporations. . . . We don't want to be out in front, to attack the establishment, to criticize major institutions, to be accused of endangering national security. . . . Sure, someone could write a two-line memo tomorrow and change the news policy of the *New York Times* to be more skeptical and challenging of established institutions. But they don't do it, not because they couldn't do it, not because they don't have the power to do it, but because they don't want to suffer more than the minimal necessary disapproval of the league of gentlemen.*

Prior to 1960, in what was still called the newspaper game, it was generally believed that reporters had more in common with vagabond poets than they did with either Rosencrantz or Guildenstern. They hired themselves out as journeymen, not as immortal artists, and they tended to identify with the crowd in the bleachers rather than with the product endorse-

---

*John Swinton, the former chief of staff at the *New York Times,* put the matter somewhat more plainly in a toast delivered to a farewell banquet in his honor at the New York Press Club in 1953:

There is no such thing, at this date, of the world's history, in America, as an independent press. . . . The business of the journalist is to destroy truth; to lie outright; to pervert; to vilify; to fawn at the feet of Mammon, and to sell his country and his race for his daily bread. You know it and I know it and what folly is this toasting an independent press? We are the tools and vassals for rich men behind the scenes. We are jumping jacks, they pull the strings and we dance. Our talents, our possibilities and our lives are all the property of other men. We are intellectual prostitutes.

Nearly fifty years later, even the intrepid Dan Rather was moved to reflect on his status as an expensive publicist. Speaking to John R. MacArthur, the publisher of *Harper's Magazine,* Rather said: "We begin to think less in terms of responsibility and integrity, which get you in trouble . . . and more in terms of power and money. . . . Increasingly anybody who subscribes to the idea that the job is not to curry favor with people you cover . . . finds himself as a kind of lone wolf. . . . Suck-up coverage is in."

ments in the box seats. None would have declared himself a gentleman, and if asked to state his occupation he would have said "reporter" or "newspaperman." The term "journalist" pertained only to Englishmen and would-be novelists, but if the scribblers at the *Examiner* in the late 1950s understood that most of the news in the paper belonged within the tradition of the old Italian *commedia dell'arte,* they also understood that against the abuses of power available to any government, the best defense is a raucous and belligerent press, its virtues inherent in its character as a necessary affliction rather than as a healing ointment. Necessary precisely because it *was* an affliction, for exactly those reasons that require of its practitioners little refinement and less compassion, no sense of aesthetics, and the gall of a coroner. Better able to diagnose than to cure, and not a fit occupation for the landed or intellectual gentry, journalism serves its most useful purpose when it presents society with the rude measure of the distance between the graceful images of an approved reality and the awkward facts of the matter; it betrays itself when it feigns diplomacy or attempts philosophy, when the scribes and pharisees construe themselves as oracles or undersecretaries of state and imagine the business of government as a stately pageant in which grave statesmen wearing white gloves pass noble documents to one another on silver trays. The courtly pretensions leech the blood out of the animal and make it an easy prey for those of its enemies who would gag its mouth with cinnamon and apples.

Not that "suck-up coverage" wasn't always in at the higher elevations of the fourth estate, but I think it probably fair to say that the toadying character of the national news media has become considerably more pronounced over the last thirty years, as much a consequence of the expansion of the national security state as of the ascendant spirit of oligarchy. John F. Kennedy's glamorous entrance onto the stage of the White House in the winter of 1961 coincided with the birth of an age in which journalists could become celebrities. The new recruits to a suddenly respectable profession brought with them from Harvard and Princeton bound volumes of the absolute truth, regarding themselves as the social equals of the politicians and movie stars about whom they were obliged to make popular romances. Most of them knew more about the pleasures of Paris or London than they did about the sorrows of Brooklyn or Newark, and quite a few of them had seen prior service as officers of the state.* The rates of pay kept pace with the expanding wealth of the communications industries, and to the extent that the gov-

---

*Even a partial list of the journalists who began their careers as government shills explains why the story of the news has lost much of its pungency and humor:

Bill Moyers—speechwriter and press secretary for President Lyndon Johnson

Diane Sawyer—speechwriter for Richard Nixon

William Safire—speechwriter for President Nixon and Vice President Spiro Agnew

David Gergen—communications director for President Ronald Reagan

Tim Russert—press aide to Senator Daniel P. Moynihan

Bob Woodward—Pentagon briefing officer to the Nixon White House

James Fallows—speechwriter for President Jimmy Carter

Patrick Buchanan—speechwriter for Presidents Richard Nixon and Ronald Reagan

ernment and the media have learned to flatter each other by promoting their mutual importance, our journalists have become increasingly vain. Given the vast increases of wealth and authority assigned to the news media over the last forty years, I don't know how or whether the temptation could have been avoided. Most of the newspapers that were once independently owned have been sold to large syndicates, and as those syndicates in turn have become fewer in number, the always narrower concentrations of wealth and decision inhibit the impulse for dissent.

As few as nine conglomerates now manufacture and distribute 90 percent of the country's news and entertainment product; three corporations (AOL, Yahoo, and Microsoft) manage 50 percent of the Internet traffic; and the Federal Communications Commission (established in 1934 to prommote "the public interest") so obviously serves private interests that in the spring and summer of 2003, when considering the latest series of rules changes (changes that further concentrated the holdings of the monopoly syndicates), it held only one public hearing—not in Washington but in Richmond, Virginia. Not surprisingly, the wealthy corporations that own and operate the media color-coordinate their editorial messages with the commercial advertising.

The ancient Romans offset the vanity of military triumph by standing a centurion in the chariot with the general riding into the city at the head of a procession of slaves, elephants, and expatriated gold. As the crowds cheered, the centurion whispered into the general's ear, "Remember you are mor-

tal." Our modern press stands behind our moneyed over-
lords and whispers, "Know that you are a god."

During the weeks leading up to George Bush's presidential nomination in the summer of 2000, the adjectives became more flattering and submissive as he approached the
rostrum in Philadelphia, the once ignorant and boorish chief-
tain from the Texas plains becoming more statesmanlike and
wise at every step, until at last, on the morning of his triumphant entrance into the city, the *New York Times* on its
front page welcomed "a man of dazzling charm, tremendous
social skills, a bold self-confidence, growing political savvy,
great popularity." Three years later the network anchor-
persons applied the same makeup to Arnold Schwarzenegger
when he accepted the news of his election to the governor-
ship of California from the perfumed hand of Jay Leno.

The American news media are the product of the American
educational system, and their unwillingness to speak for
themselves (in Archibald MacLeish's phrase, "to resign,"
even momentarily, "from the herd") should come as no surprise. The dumbing down of the schools is neither an acci-
dent nor a mistake. We are a people blessed with a genius for
large organizational tasks, and if we were serious in our
pious mumbling about the need for educational reform—
if we honestly believed that mind took precedence over
money—our schools surely would stand as the eighth wonder of the world. But we neither like nor trust the forces of

intellect—not unless they can be securely fixed to a commercial profit or an applied technology—and if most of what passes for education in the United States deadens the desire for learning, the miserable result accurately reflects the miserable intent.

No American schoolmaster ever outlined the lesson at hand quite as plainly as Woodrow Wilson. While he was still president of Princeton University, Wilson in 1909 presented the Federation of High School Teachers with explicit instructions: "We want one class of persons to have a liberal education, and we want another class of persons, a very much larger class of necessity in every society, to forgo the privilege of a liberal education and fit themselves to perform specific difficult manual tasks."

The pedagogues of Wilson's generation recognized the possibility of unrest implicit in a too-well-educated electorate, and they took it upon themselves to rig the curricula in a way that discouraged the habits of skepticism or dissent. Redefining democracy as "primarily a mode of associated living" (as opposed to a belief in liberty), they argued that American schools should cut the cloth of their teaching to what John Dewey called "the circumstances, needs and opportunities of industrial civilization." They had in mind the training of a contented labor force, prospective members of the national economic team, "socially efficient" workers who understood that what was great about America was the greatness of its gross national product and not the greatness of its character and spirit. The revised lesson plan displaced the older republican hope of a citizenry schooled to the task of self-government. Jefferson had urged the teaching of political history so that Americans might learn "how to judge for themselves what will secure or endanger their freedom"; John Adams had seconded the motion, observing that "[a free people has] an indisputable, unalienable, indefeasible, divine right to that most dreaded and envied kind of knowledge, I mean of the characters and conduct of their rulers."

The corporate managers of the Bush administration classify their characters and conduct as a state secret, and they take considerable pains to conceal from a nominally free people any and all knowledge apt to excite not only envy and dread but also reasonable doubt and faint suspicion.* Nor do they have much use for citizens, especially citizens likely to see the would-be despot behind the mask of the popular general or the avuncular judge. Jefferson had asked, in effect, how free men could protect their liberties if they never learned that it was the business of most politicians to remove those liberties. The Wilson administration subtracted a good many liberties from the public domain during the First World War, and its Committee on Public Information invented the syllabus of the great books of Western civiliza-

---

*The Justice Department encourages its operatives to deny all requests presented under the Freedom of Information Act; President Bush has placed all White House papers, his own as well as those of his father, under the seal of secrecy; fearful of listening devices and of secretaries taking notes, the upper servants of the Bush administration arrange to talk to one another while standing next to the sound of running water or helicopter engines. Vice President Dick Cheney's office imposes on its clerks and policy intellectuals the Mafia rule of *omertà*.

tion (aka "the canon") as a means of quieting what a dean at
Columbia University called "the destructive element in our
society," to produce students who "shall be safe for democracy" and to make of the American troops in France what
History Teachers' Magazine called "thinking bayonets."

The difficulty, as Wilson well and clearly understood, was
political. How do you teach people to "judge for themselves
what will secure or endanger their freedom" unless you also
teach them how to think? And if you teach too many people
how to think, then how can you be sure that they won't ask
the wrong questions? Why would any politician wish to confront an informed citizenry that could read the federal
budget, decipher the news from Washington, and break
down the election-year images into their subsets of compo-
nent lies? Why would the purveyors of American goods and
services choose to afflict themselves with a public intelligent
enough to find the hidden interest rates or see through the
scrim of the four-color advertisements? The success of the
American dream, like the success of MasterCard and the Republican Party, presupposes the eager and uncritical con-
sumption of junk in all its commercial declensions. Teach
people to think for themselves and maybe they won't buy the
deodorant or the perfume, or believe that the glorious victory in Baghdad proves the need for a newer and more expensive collection of tanks. So troublesome a person might
even bother to vote.

Because the schools serve an economic system rather
than a political or philosophical idea, they promote, not unreasonably, the habits of mind necessary to the preservation

of that system, which is why an American education resembles the commercial procedure that changes caterpillars into silkworms instead of butterflies. Silkworms can be turned to a profit, but butterflies blow around in the wind and do nothing to add to the wealth of the corporation or the power of the state. An inept and insolent bureaucracy armed with badly written textbooks instills in the class the attitudes of passivity, compliance, and boredom, and if the public schools employ the punitive devices of overcrowded classrooms, recitations by rote, questions shaped to the simple answer of yes or no, they do so because they aspire to the recidivism rates of successful penal institutions. Our students major in the arts of failure and the science of diminished expectation.*

It's probably fair to say that as a society we lay waste every year to roughly 70 percent of our intellectual capacity, and that outside the classroom as well as in, the never-ending war against the American intellect returns as handsome a profit as the never-ending war on terror. The reservoirs of ignorance and superstition count as a natural resource of greater

---

*Some years ago in *Harper's Magazine* I published a few melancholy notes about the reduced circumstances of our political discourse, and from a woman in Maryland I received a stern reminder to the effect that the fault, dear Brutus, was not in our stars. "We do not," she wrote, "ask nearly enough of ourselves—not of parents, not of children, not of women, not of men, not of our institutions, not of our talents, not of our national or our personal character, not of our Constitution's promise, which we betray." In that one sentence she said most of what needs to be said about the emptiness of the nation's politics and the shabbiness of the nation's schools.

consequence to the gross domestic product than the amber waves of grain, and for the manufacturers of political and sexual fantasy the electronic forms of communication have proved to be as much of a blessing as the bountiful wilderness discovered by the early settlers on the shores of seventeenth-century New England. Marshall McLuhan's *Understanding Media: The Extensions of Man* mapped the new landscape in 1964, describing it as "an acoustic world, one with no continuity, no stasis, which comes at us from all directions . . . a totally new information environment of which humanity has never had any experience whatever." A Canadian professor of what was then known as "pop culture," fond of distributing oracular statements and adamantly opposed to "all innovation, all change," McLuhan regarded himself as a prophet bearing bad news, not unlike Cassandra foretelling the ruin of ancient Troy. Framing his observations on the premise "We shape our tools and thereafter our tools shape us," he proceeded to an analogy between the fifteenth-century invention of movable type and the nineteenth-century invention of the electric lightbulb. Content follows form; "we become what we behold," and new systems of communication give rise to new structures of feeling and thought. Just as the printing press incited a revolution that overturned a settled aesthetic and political order, the practical applications of electricity—as telephone, telegraph, computer, movie camera, and television screen—remanded to oblivion any and all prior definitions of reality. The visual structure of the printed page supports a perception of the world biased in favor of sequence, roads, narrative, hierarchy, classification, straight lines. Glimpses of the world derived from the electronic media shape a sensibility geared to improvisation, circles, discontinuity, repetition, simultaneity, and incantation. The habits of mind associated with the rule of images destroy the civilization dependent on the meaning of words.

Neither McLuhan's admirers nor his critics took him at his word. Even as he passed across the zenith of his fame in the late 1960s, he was mistaken for a dealer in exotic aphorisms and rare conundrums—"the electric light is pure information," "we are the television screen . . . we wear all mankind as our skin." Woody Allen placed him on the set of *Annie Hall,* Andy Warhol appointed him to the office of honorary muse, and during the five or six years in which his Delphic utterance remained in vogue, fumblers after the season's stylish truth in both *Harper's Bazaar* and the *New York Review of Books* relied upon the magical word "McLuhanesque" to explain otherwise inexplicable moral and cultural phenomena.

The excitements associated with *Understanding Media* didn't survive its author's death in 1980, and as perhaps was to be expected from craftsmen still working in a medium that the decedent had declared extinct, the obituary notices were less than kind. McLuhan's prophecies were sent to the attic with the go-go boots, and the once foremost oracle of an age was demoted to the rank of harmless lunatic. The judgment was poorly timed. Much of what McLuhan had to say makes a good deal more sense in the twenty-first century than it did in the twentieth, his prescience become manifest

in cyberspace by the instruments (fiber optics, satellite television, CD-ROM, and the Internet) that he didn't live to see
shaped in silicon and glass.

As recently as 1960 it was still possible to make distinctions between the several variations of what were then
known as the lively arts, the several audiences recognizing
the differences among journalism, literature, politics, and the
movies. The distinctions blurred under the technical and
epistemological pressures of the next ten years, and as the
lines between fact and fiction became as irrelevant as they
were difficult to distinguish, the lively arts fused into the
amalgam of forms known as the media. News was entertainment, entertainment was news; the special effects were
astonishing, and by 1980 the theater of celebrity had replaced
the old mythical amphitheater in which Poseidon and Zeus
once staged cataclysmic floods and heavenly fires with the
effortless aplomb of ABC's *Wide World of Sports.*

By eliminating the dimensions of space and time, the accelerated data streams of the electronic media also eliminate
the association of cause with effect, and in what McLuhan
came to see as both "the global village" and "the pool of
Narcissus," the time is always now. Spin the merry-go-round
of the automatous media in such a way that all the world's joy
and all the world's sorrow are always and everywhere present
(if not on channel 4 in New York or Los Angeles, then on
channels 27 and 41 in London or Rangoon; if not on
CNN or *Oprah,* then on the Saturday Night Movie, at www.
whitehouse.gov, or at a 900 number answering to the name

of Domino), and the solo voice of the unaffiliated and unorthodox individual sinks into the chorus of a corporate
consciousness that, as McLuhan had foreseen, "doesn't pos-
tulate consciousness of anything in particular."

Nor does the usage of the perpetual present tense lend
itself to the expression of dissent, a form of argument
grounded, like the essay, the novel, and the Supreme Court
ruling, on the visual order of print. In place of narrative the
electronic media provide montage; the rules of grammar and
syntax give way to an arrangement of rebuses like those
made from the flashing signs in Times Square. Nothing necessarily follows from anything else; sequence becomes merely
additive instead of causative—the images bereft of memory,
speaking to their own reflections in a vocabulary better
suited to the sale of a product than to the articulation of a
thought.

The point was never better illustrated than on September 11, 2002, in New York City by the pageant commemo-
rating the first anniversary of America's lost innocence. The
lead editorial in that morning's *Daily News* spoke to the difficulty of the performance—"What can be said that hasn't
been said? What can be written that hasn't been written?" It
wasn't that the city lacked for citizens capable of both high-
end philosophy and noble speech, but so many people were
presenting so many shows of grief or patriotism that the vast
cloud of inchoate emotion drifting through the streets and
across the television screens suppressed, with the rhetorical
equivalents of tear gas, even the most stubborn attempts to

make sense of the occasion. So much was being said or seen that nothing could be heard.*

The audible silence conformed to Mayor Michael R. Bloomberg's wish that everybody celebrating his or her status as a victim must be made to "feel comfortable." The city had gone to no small trouble or expense to mount a production comparable to Bono's Super Bowl halftime show, and the municipal authorities had been careful to defend the speakers' platforms against any sudden outbreaks of meaning. The dignitaries invited to approach the microphones at Ground Zero came with the understanding that they were to say nothing controversial or insensitive, to bring no statements stained with vile political content, to let fall no offhand remarks that might be mistaken for tasteless irony or bitter truth. In compliance with the security precautions, they confined their oratory to ritual incantation, reciting selected paragraphs from the Declaration of Independence, reading the names of those who perished in the ruin of the World Trade Center, declaiming the Gettysburg Address.

---

*In place of words the event planners offered images, multicultural and generic, expressive of anything and everything the spectators chose to see, wish for, or believe—moments of silence interspersed with the tolling of church bells, a scattering of roses and the trembling of candlelight, the Wiping Away Tears ritual performed by a troupe of Native Americans, Yo-Yo Ma playing the "Ave Maria" on the cello, a groundbreaking for the Garden of Healing on Staten Island, numerous exhibits of melancholy photographs and inspirational quilts, the chanting of Buddhist monks cross-promoted with the murmuring of Catholic priests, firehouse chalkboards displayed at the Metropolitan Museum of Art, and the bookstores selling out their inventories of *Chicken Soup for the Soul of America.*

Elsewhere in the city, the celebrity witnesses granted access to a television camera seldom failed to glimpse a phoenix rising from the ashes of destruction, and although some of them pretended to a close acquaintance with the miraculous bird, they unfailingly associated it with the American spirit, eagle feathered and indomitable, shining with a renewed sense of national unity and purpose. Given the solemnity of the occasion, it was impossible to doubt the truth of their emotion. What was more difficult to judge was the future they had in mind. Almost as soon as they had said that America would never again be the same, they began to talk about the restoration of a familiar and heroic past, making good the casualties of September 11 with quicker-witted intelligence agents, longer-range artillery, more patriotic displays of consumer confidence in all the nation's better stores. If the fine words didn't amount to much when measured for their weight of meaning, possibly it was because the finding of a phoenix in the ashes presupposes the use of a language free of cowardice, and on the first anniversary of the calamity in Lower Manhattan most of the public or quasi-public figures likely to appear before an American microphone no longer possessed such a language.

Citizens marooned in the suburbs could turn instead to a long day's festival of television programming, ninety hours of it as dedicated as Mayor Bloomberg to the proposition that every demographic division of the audience must feel comfortable in the warm baths of market-tested sentiment. Not wishing to be thought vulgar or exploitive, wealthy corporations (among them Coca-Cola, General Motors, and

American Airlines) refrained from all forms of advertising between the hours of dawn and dusk; the network and cable broadcasts made such sparing use of "traumatic" or "assaultive" footage that the destruction of the World Trade Center was transported into the realm of delicate and remote metaphor, the damage merely hinted at with brief glimpses of a burning building or a falling man, with fragmentary wisps of smoke and fleeting, sidelong glances at the face of death or pain. Tom Brokaw, on the verge of tears, listened sympathetically to the tales of loss and remembrance; Diane Sawyer dandled an orphan on her knee; a PBS documentary asked, "Where was God on September 11?" and answered the question in words suitable for stitching on a throw pillow; from Ellis Island just after sunset, posed against the backdrop of the Statue of Liberty, President Bush called on God to "see us through" and so preserve America as "the hope of all mankind" and the light that "shines in the darkness." The day ended in an attitude of prayer, but it was by no means easy to know to whom, or for what, the congregation prayed. So many symbols had been paraded through the streets and displayed in the show windows of the television screen that the significance of the spectacle remained open to interpretation.

Blessed with a system of knowledge that grants priority to the comfort of the inward feeling rather than to the possible embarrassment of the observed fact, we can listen to the Gettysburg Address in the same way that we listen to elevator music. We don't hear what the words say or mean, but they evoke a pleasing mood, soft and elegiac, into which we can fit a memory of anything that comes easily to mind—the teacher's bright blue dress on the day when we first saw Abraham Lincoln's picture in a fourth-grade history book, leaves scattering across Grandmother's porch in an autumn wind, the ice-cream man in the candy-striped coat on the lawn near the Washington Monument.

Who would want it otherwise, and why get off the couch? Here we all are living more or less happily ever after within the virtual reality provided by a news and entertainment media that can reconfigure death as a sales pitch for a weapons budget or a face cream. In the climate-controlled atmosphere under the dome of brightly packaged images floating over the stadium of the national consciousness, we rely on the technical staff to repair any structural damage caused by low-flying aircraft or the weather—to plug the holes, fix the leaks, seal the cracks with quilts and Mozart's Requiem.

Fill up the dome with a sufficient volume of cultural product, and nobody needs to find new words with which to tell a new story. A brave man on a hijacked plane says to his fellow passengers, "Let's roll," and within a matter of weeks the phrase shows up as a Neil Young song, a bestselling T-shirt, the motto of a president's speech to Congress, a college cheer for a Florida football team. The instant recognition of a familiar pattern stands as a synonym for wisdom (wised-up, in the know, party to the joke), and the striking of a pose serves as an analogue for thought. We need only learn how to recycle last year's earthquake into next year's movie, when to change a Hollywood action hero into a governor of California, how and where to shop for the future rather than go to the trouble of making it. To deepen character, add accessories.

The news coverage of Operation Iraqi Freedom filled up the stadium dome with adult entertainment product, X-rated instead of PG-13, the broadcasts from the fog of war as incessant as the bombing raids on Baghdad, deaf to the hope of a coherent narrative. The twenty-four-hour montage on the cable channels resembled the dream sequences of a commercial for men's cologne. The misinformation and the disinformation were so deftly intercut with the front-line first impressions, the images so quickly revised, repeated, updated, cross-promoted, or shifted to another camera angle (mortar rounds entering stage left, an artillery barrage exiting stage right, two- and three-star generals parading to and fro on Tom Brokaw's reviewing stand, the correspondent aboard an aircraft carrier handing the microphone across a split screen to the correspondent embedded in a Bradley fighting vehicle) that before the invasion was two days north of Umm Qasr the accelerated data stream was as impenetrable as the sandstorm descending on the Third Infantry Division's auxiliary helicopters. The computer animations of the weapons systems and the tactical movements looked like video games, the "virtual views" of the topography like the golf-course graphics deployed to illustrate the perils of the PGA Tour, and the fireworks display over old, romantic Baghdad inspired heroic feats of merchandising not only on the part of the Pentagon and White House briefing officers but also among the manufacturers of cigars and women's underwear, their flurry of applications for the trademark

"Shock and Awe" competing with those submitted by the makers of doll-house furnishings, ski boots, mouse pads, teddy bears, smoking jackets, yo-yos, and inflatable bathtub toys.

The postmodern imagination is a product of the mass media, but as a means of perception it is more accurately described as pre-Christian. The vocabulary is necessarily primitive, reducing argument to gossip and history to the telling of fairy tales. The more efficient and expensive the machinery, the poorer and smaller the meaning. The future comes and goes as quickly as the past, before anybody has time to remember what it was supposed to be about, and the news appears as such a familiar ritual—the same footage, the same words, the same official spokesman—that we know that what was said last week will be said again this week, and then next week, and once again six weeks from now. Like the old pagan systems of belief, the electronic media grant the primacy of the personal over the impersonal, and whether in Washington hearing rooms or Hollywood restaurants, names take precedence over things, the actors over the acts. On television commercials and subway signs, celebrities of various magnitude, like the nymphs and satyrs and fauns of ancient myth, become the familiar spirits of automobiles, cameras, computers, and brokerage firms. Athletes show up on television breathing the gift of life into whatever products can be carried into a locker room; aging movie actresses awaken with their "personal touch" the spirit dormant in a lipstick or a cell phone. Just as the ancient Greeks assigned trace elements of the divine to trees and winds and stones (a river god sulked and the child drowned; a sky god smiled and the corn ripened), the modern American assigns similar powers not only to whales and Giorgio Armani but also to Arnold Schwarzenegger and spotted owls.

The technology favors the presentation of the national political argument as a Punch and Judy show—on stage left a motley crew of liberal-minded people allied with the yearnings of the human spirit and the mechanics of social reform, on stage right a military formation of conservative-minded people who stand, foursquare and all-American, for the sanctity of property and the punishment of scoundrels. Under the old rules of rhetoric allied with the parliamentary order of print, the proceedings make no sense. The meanings of the words "liberal" and "conservative" have been so mercilessly abused over the last twenty years that they offer more information about the person who employs them as insults than they do about the person on whose head they fall like stones. To say that A is liberal or B conservative is to say nothing intelligible about his or her politics, conduct, occupation, place of residence, or record of prior arrests. It is conceivable, even likely, that the woman identified as a liberal thinks nothing of tapping her daughter's telephone and enjoys an after-tax income of $2 million a year supplied by eight-year-old seamstresses earning three dollars a day in a Chinese cellar. On the opposite side of the stereotype, it is equally conceivable that the man labeled as a conservative devotes his life and fortune to the protection of hummingbirds and refuses to eat grapes picked by nonunion Mexican field hands.

As negative caricatures, however, the words retain a high-definition theatrical value for the troupe of polemicists seeking to lend gravitas to the pages of *The Nation* and the *National Review*. The antiliberal prides himself on the clarity of his intellect. When talking about the faculty of intelligence (his own or that of his friends, associates, and Paul Wolfowitz), he invariably describes it as "ruthless" or "unrelenting." Believing that he has seen through the veils of sentimental illusion, he talks incessantly about "reality" and what things cost, about the way in which deluded technocrats persist in confusing the Kingdom of Heaven with a socialist welfare state. Sooner or later he gets around to saying that there isn't enough money in the world, and he can be counted upon to draw the comparison between the Yale English Department and the Gulag Archipelago. The anticonservative prides himself on the quality of his emotions. A Canadian poet of his acquaintance supplies him with bootleg metaphor, and he believes that he has looked into the bottomless well of human suffering. He talks about "moral parameters" and what things mean, about Calvinism made abominable, and Republicans as landlords undeservedly rich and prematurely old. Sooner or later he gets around to saying that there isn't enough love in the world, and he can be counted upon to draw the comparison between Orange County and Nazi Germany. Given the stupidities of the American government and the inequities of the country's socioeconomic seating plan, both the antiliberal and the anticonservative find proofs of their worst suspicions in every morning's newspaper. The prerecorded argument, as loud as possible and heavily embellished with references to the apocalypse, sells books, brings lecture fees, threatens nobody.

The last and most obstinate of the impediments in the way of forceful political dissent is what Walter Karp understood to be the "corrupting consolation of cynicism." Karp employed the phrase to describe the attitude of mind adopted by a generation of American intellectuals responding to the Wilson administration's harsh suppression of unlicensed speech during and after World War I. Finding themselves suffocated by a climate of opinion in which dissent was disloyalty and disloyalty a crime, a good many independent-minded and once outspoken citizens acquired the habit of looking at the national political scene from the point of view of spectators at a tenement fire or a train wreck. As compensation for their loss of a public voice, they retired to a library or a lawn party and there contented themselves with private and literary expressions of anger and disgust. Language served as an end in itself, the imagination a vehicle for escaping reality rather than a means of grasping or apprehending it.

The attitude is one that I've encountered often enough in myself to recognize in other people—not only among the card-carrying members of the country's various intellectual guilds but also among the well-to-do gentry content to leave the business of government to the hired help. Our schools teach marketing instead of history, and the prosperity of the last thirty years has encouraged a disdain for politics on the part of people who imagine that liberty is an asset inherited at birth—together with the grandfather clock and the house on the lake—rather than the product of hard and constant labor.* The universities don't take the trouble to correct the mistake. When traveling to Dartmouth or Stanford or the University of Michigan, I expect to meet people who can afford to say what they think. I find instead a faculty preoccupied with the great questions of tenure and publication. Everybody is studying the art of writing grant proposals or the forms of courteous address appropriate to the magnificence of the department chairman. The freedom of expression proves to be contingent on the circumstance—permissible in some company, not in other. In the same way that the media measure their self-esteem by the degrees of access to im-

---

*Among eligible voters in their twenties, only 13 percent cast ballots in the 2000 presidential election; no more than 50 percent believed that voting was important; 60 percent didn't know how or when or by whom the United States had been brought into existence. The official estimate of illiterate American citizens now stands at 40 million, but because the statistics measure little except the capacity to read road signs and restaurant menus, the number is optimistically low. Complicate the proceedings by one or two degrees of further comprehension (an acquaintance with a minimal number of standard texts, the capacity to recognize a tone of irony) and the number of people impaired by a lack of literary intelligence probably comes nearer to 100 million.

As many as six out of ten American adults have never read a book of any kind, and the bulletins from the nation's educational frontiers read like the casualty reports from a lost war. The witnesses tell mournful stories about polls showing that one quarter of the adults interviewed were ignorant of the news that the earth revolves around the sun, about the majority of college freshmen (68 percent) who have trouble finding California on a map, about the high school girl who thought the Holocaust was a Jewish holiday.

portant government officials, the academy depends upon its access to the media (the prestigious literary reviews, the op-ed pages of the *New York Times,* the *Washington Post,* and the *Wall Street Journal*) for the currencies of name and reputation. As with the professors, so also with the students. God forbid that they should misplace the Rolodex or omit a single move while making their way around the Monopoly board of the high end of American success. A generation ago the graduates of the country's upscale universities might have mentioned the name of a dead poet, or said something about truth and its untimely betrayals. Not now. Not when they think that if they miss their first and maybe only chance at the brass ring, they might never find their way back to the putting greens of Fairfield County or the music on the beach at Malibu.

The breaking up of the curriculum into the subsections of special interest (cultural and political as well as sexual, racial, and socioeconomic) leads to the invention of a thousand jargons in which the parties of mutually assured sentiment speak chiefly to themselves. By 1990 at many of the nation's right-thinking universities the novels of Jane Austen and George Eliot had been placed in the custody of the Department of Women's Studies, the texts subject to explication only by female professors of literature. When Spike Lee released his movie *Malcolm X* in 1992, he expressed his wish to grant interviews only to those newspapers that sent a reporter who was black. A parallel line of argument sustained the claque of Republican critics that forced CBS to cancel the broadcast of its docudrama *The Reagans* in November

2003. The actor James Brolin had been hired to play the part
of the former president, and because Brolin is married to
Barbra Streisand—notorious liberal, friend to Bill Clinton,
avowed hater of Republicans—Brolin clearly came to the set
with vicious intent. How could it not be so? The man was
marked by the company he kept, and "what cruelty must lie
in the hearts of CBS executives" to sit a Communist on the
Gipper's horse?

None of the critics had seen the four-hour movie that
served as the occasion for their alarm; their complaints arose
from rumors published in the *New York Times* on October 21,
four weeks before the dramatization of Reagan's life and
love story was scheduled to air. The producers were said to
have intended a heartwarming biography—young actor rises
to fame and fortune in Hollywood, finds God and an adoring wife, enters politics, moves upward to the White House,
and saves the country from poverty and fools—but the
screenwriters apparently had blotted their pages with a few
careless lines of dialogue suggesting weevils in the ointment
and flies in the milk. The first rumors—of scenes depicting
Reagan as an intolerant homophobe guided by the wisdom
of his wife's astrologer—were amplified by a second edition
of rumors seeping into the Internet with the Drudge Reports
of October 24 and 26—scenes depicting Reagan as a man
who confused himself with the Antichrist, and Nancy as an
angry dwarf screaming insults at the White House wine
steward. It didn't matter that in the source materials the producers could show probable cause for the complications of
character; nor did it matter that Reagan emerged at the end

of four hours as a heroic president who had restored America's faith in itself and won through to victory in the cold war against the Russians. What mattered was the network's failure to deify Reagan. The man deserved an image made of gold; any hint of imperfection implied not only carelessness but blasphemy.

On more than one occasion in New York City over the last few years, while taking part in a public discussion of American foreign policy toward Israel, I've been informed by members of the audience that my opinions on the subject were worthless because I was not a Jew. When George Soros on November 5, 2003, informed an audience of Jewish philanthropists in New York that in Europe "there is a resurgence of anti-Semitism" and that the policies of the Bush administration "contribute to that," his remarks were denounced, within a matter of days, by Congressman Eliot Engel (D.-N.Y.) as "ridiculous and outrageous" and "morally reprehensible."

Like all taboos, the one forbidding criticism of Israel defends the past against the future. The Pentagon's cadre of high-ranking geopolitical stategists consists largely of fierce and visionary ideologues who make little distinction between the objectives of the Bush administration in Washington and those of the Sharon government in Jerusalem, but requests for further clarification—and possibly a way out of the maze of bloodshed—invite the charge of bigotry. Jews who ask questions find themselves modified by the adjective "self-hating."

The rendering of politics as fashion statement no doubt can be understood as proof of the country's immense wealth and as a tribute to the success of its experiments with virtual reality, but it fosters a habit of mind unable to imagine a future that doesn't resemble a Hollywood remake or a Broadway revival. The circumstance explains the political ignorance of the New York literary salons. The subjects under discussion require too detailed a knowledge of history, law, finance, or nuclear physics, which in turn bear witness to the world's rigor and complexity—distasteful and faintly vulgar. Far better to strike moral or aesthetic poses and so concentrate on the recognition (or, more often, nonrecognition) of mutual states of refined feeling.* Why make trouble? Why argue with the system that provides one with a microphone, a syndication deal, and a hairstylist? Learn to confine the expression of dissent to the wearing of an angry nose ring, and look for a better world in the lands of fantasy and irony.

---

*I suspect that, if asked to fill out a passport application stating their country of residence or origin, a good many writers of my own age and generation might identify themselves not as Americans but as Utopians or Counterrevolutionaries, possibly as Southerners or Catholics, but always as discerning visitors from a better world (frequently confused with their childhoods), passing through town on their way to Scotland. Their detachment is partly a matter of literary convention. The modernist doctrines taught in the schools over the last twenty or thirty years require the writer with pretensions to sensibility to conceive of the world as a metaphor. Tom Clancy might still take the trouble to explain the workings of an automobile or a weapons factory, but the writer who aspires to keep company with the immortals learns to affect a well-bred ignorance of politics and trade.

The willingness to go along to get along is as American as the Salem witch trials and apple pie. Alexis de Tocqueville remarked on the prevalence of what he called "the courtier spirit" in the United States when passing through Nashville, Tennessee, in the winter of 1831. He had thought that the citizens of a new democracy would prove to be turbulent and rough-hewn people, direct in their actions and forthright in their speech. He was surprised to find them so seldom inclined to exercise their well-advertised freedom of expression. True, they didn't dress as well as the ladies and gentlemen in France; their conversation wasn't as refined, and neither were their manners; but they possessed a marvelous talent for ingratiating themselves with anyone who could do them a service or a favor. Worried about losing a fraction of an advantage or a degree of self-importance, they were very, very careful about talking out of turn, and it occurred to Tocqueville that never in his travels had he encountered a people so easily cowed by the "tyranny of the majority" and so desirous of being perceived as "polite."*

---

*The observation speaks to the American fear of being found out. To a greater or lesser degree, we are all impostors, self-invented people, con artists afraid that somebody will call our bluff, see through the disguise, send for the IRS agents or the police. Expressions of dissent run the risk of being mistaken for personal insults, which might arouse suspicion and so lead to the loss of an identity that we define as an economic rather than a political construct. Even when we know that we're being told a handsome lie by a mutal fund manager or the president of the United States, we tip our hat to the semblance of integrity and wait to consume the eventual discovery of fraud as the next year's bestselling scandal.

In all its tenses and declensions (some complacent and luxurious, others bitter and ascetic) the corrupting consolation of cynicism is the cynical politician's most precious asset and truest friend. Yes, say the gentlemen in power, exactly right, the world is a terrible place, overflowing with terrorists and swindlers, and you, my dear fellow, you are so sensitive and smart that it would be a crime to squander your talent in the sewer of politics, to do anything else but sit here in the garden with the novels of Marcel Proust. Do nothing, they say, because you might get hurt, if not by a nuclear weapon or a bus then by a polluted trout or a collapsing dollar; serve the apples with the cheese, feed the canary, sail away to Peru with Patrick O'Brian's masters and commanders. We would do the same if only we had the chance, but we're not so insightful as you, not so well read or profound, and so we must leave tonight for London to talk to an Arab about a bomb.

The reassurances are as false as the disinformation circulated by the publicists at the Pentagon, and they speak to the point made by J. M. Coetzee in *Waiting for the Barbarians:* "One thought alone preoccupies the submerged mind of Empire: how not to end, how not to die, how to prolong its era." The Bush administration's imbecile realpolitik derives from the submerged jealousy of a future apt to render its principal ornaments ridiculous, and when I listen to President Bush and Secretary Rumsfeld threaten the wind in the trees and the shadows on the sea, I remember the story about a French noblewoman, a duchess in her eighties, who, on seeing the ascent of the Montgolfiers' balloon from the Bois de Boulogne in 1783, fell back upon the cushions of her carriage and wept. "Oh, yes," she said, "now it's certain. One day they'll learn how to keep people alive forever, but I shall already be dead."

Certainly it is futile to expect anything more of the world than it has the capacity to produce, and probably it is pointless to deplore the failures and shortcomings of people trying to get by as best they know how. What can anybody ask of authority except that it make a credible show of itself? Civil magistrates, as well as corporation presidents, need as much help as they can get, and if they shore themselves up with whatever pomps and hypocrisies come easily to hand, why begrudge them their traffic in propaganda? If the fabric of authority is torn by revolution, then another tapestry made of the same poor stuff must, of necessity, replace it.

Even so, and then possibly in only very small amounts, the truth is precious. People who tell themselves too many lies ("When I am elected . . . ," "When your grandmother dies . . . ," "When my wife gives me a divorce . . .") commit a form of suicide. So do governments that encourage their citizens to stupefy themselves with drugs, luxury, superstition, and a steady supply of digitally enhanced pornography. The Old Man of the Mountains made his followers smoke hashish in order to convert them into assassins.

Several years ago on its editorial page the *New York Times* issued the complacent announcement that "great publications magnify beyond measure the voice of any single writer." The sentence employed the wrong verb. The instruments of the media multiply or amplify a voice, serving much the same purpose as a loudspeaker in a ballpark or a prison. What magnifies a voice is its wisdom and compassion, and against the weight of the world's iniquity the best resource is the imaginative labor of trying to tell the truth. Not an easy task, but the courage required of the writer, if he or she seriously attempts it—and the response called forth in the reader, if he or she recognizes the attempt as an honest one—increases the common stores of energy and hope.*

*In *The American Democrat,* published in 1838, James Fenimore Cooper argued that the word "American" was synonymous with the habit of telling the truth:

> By candor we are not to understand trifling and uncalled for exposition of truth; but a sentiment that poses a conviction of the necessity of speaking truth, and speaking it all. . . . The public has a right to be treated with candor. Without this manly and truly republican quality . . . the institutions are converted into a stupendous fraud.

FOUR

Democracy in Irons

They that can give up essential liberties to obtain a little
temporary safety deserve neither liberty nor safety.

—BENJAMIN FRANKLIN

The publication of Tom Paine's *Common Sense* in January
1776 kindled the spark of the American Revolution, but the
victory at Yorktown in October 1781 brought its author little else except the prize of unemployment. The incendiary
polemic had proved useful to rebellious colonists looking for
a worthy cause; so had Paine's binding up of the wounds of
American defeat in battle with the composition of *The Crisis
Papers* that were passed from hand to hand around military
campfires at Saratoga and Valley Forge—"These are the
times that try men's souls"; "What we obtain too cheap, we
esteem too lightly"; "Virtue is not hereditary." The peace
settlement killed the market for dissent. Once again understood as a bad career move, unseemly displays of candor
reemerged as blotches on the smiling face of ambition; no

longer was there any profit to be gained from the circulation of possibly unsanitary truths. To the propertied gentry in Massachusetts and New York, Paine stood revealed as an idealist unfitted to the work of dividing up the spoils—a man too much given to plain speaking, on too-familiar terms with the lower orders of society and therefore not to be trusted.

The reformulated set of circumstances declared Paine's rhetoric superfluous, his services no longer required by the lace-ruffled politicians, men like John Jay and Gouverneur Morris, who feared the "democratic rabble" in the streets of Philadelphia and thought that the newly acquired American estate should be governed by the gentlemen who owned it. Denied political appointment by an ungrateful Congress, the progenitor of the American War of Independence sailed for Europe in 1787, still bent on his great project of political transformation and social change. In England he wrote *The Rights of Man,* the book in which he sought to give programmatic form to his plan for a just society and which, 150 years ahead of its time, anticipates much of the legislation that eventually showed up in the United States under the rubrics of Franklin Roosevelt's New Deal—government welfare payments to the poor, pensions for the elderly, public funding of education, reductions of military spending, a tax limiting the amount of an inheritance. The book appeared in two volumes in 1791–92; the sale of five hundred thousand copies ranked it the bestselling book of the entire eighteenth century and prompted the British government to charge the author with treason and to declare him an outlaw.*

Paine left for France in the summer of 1792, to find a joyous crowd of newly enfranchised citizens according him a hero's welcome on the waterfront at Calais. To the makers of the French Revolution, *The Rights of Man* bore the stamps of hope and freedom, and as testimony of their appreciation they promptly elected Paine to the political assembly then at work in Paris on the construction of yet another new republic. He remained in France for the rest of the century, arrested by Robespierre's Committee of Public Safety when the revolution degenerated into the Reign of Terror, writing the second volume of *The Age of Reason* while in the Luxembourg prison awaiting a summons to the guillotine. Together with Voltaire and Benjamin Franklin, Paine became one of the most famous and best-loved figures of the Enlightenment. Napoleon Bonaparte thought him the great contemporary apostle of liberty, fraternity, and equality to whom there "ought to be erected," in every city in the universe, "a statue of gold."

The opinion was not shared by the Federalist Party that had come to power in America during the decade of the 1790s. John Adams's summing up of Paine's character— "a mongrel between pig and puppy, begotten by a wild boar on a bitch wolf"—strikes the tone of an editorial in the *Wall*

---

*Stylish British aristocrats struck coins in Paine's image so that they might affix them to the heels of their boots and thus grind into dust the face of the author of *The Rights of Man* while walking to and fro on the cobblestone streets of London.

Street Journal deploring a novel by Susan Sontag or the draft of a health care bill proposed by Senator Ted Kennedy. To listen to Vice President Dick Cheney telling NBC News that neither the American Congress nor the American people have the right to pry into the government's secrets (not only with regard to what it knows or doesn't know about Iraqi weapons of mass destruction but also in regard to its alliances with Saudi Arabia and the Bechtel Corporation), is to hear the echo of Adams complaining of "those little busy meddling scribblers that are always buzzing about the press in America."

Scorned by an American government that Thomas Jefferson characterized as "a reign of witches," Paine wouldn't have had much trouble recognizing the Bush administration as Federalist in sentiment, "monarchical" and "aristocratical" in its actions, royalist in its mistrust of freedom, imperialist in the bluster of its military pretensions, evangelical in its worship of property. In the White House we have a president appointed by the Supreme Court; at the Justice Department, an attorney general who believes that in America "there is no king but Jesus"; in both houses of Congress, a corpulent majority that votes its allegiance to class privilege and hereditary virtue. The natural tendency of such a government to collapse into the rubble of tyranny furnished Paine with the theme for which he found variations in all of his writing. From Paris in 1796, in an open letter to President George Washington that was published in a Philadelphia newspaper, he remarked on the fate likely to befall a republic bereft of both its principles and its senses:

When we contemplate the fall of empires and the extinction of the nations of the Ancient World, we see but little to excite our regret than the mouldering ruins of pompous palaces, magnificent museums, lofty pyramids and walls and towers of the most costly workmanship; but when the empire of America shall fall, the subject for contemplative sorrow will be infinitely greater than crumbling brass and marble can inspire. It will not then be said, here stood a temple of vast antiquity; here rose a Babel of invisible height; or there a palace of sumptuous extravagance; but here, Ah, painful thought! The noblest work of human wisdom, the grandest scene of human glory, the fair cause of Freedom rose and fell.*

---

*Thirty-six years later, in a speech marking the one hundredth anniversary of George Washington's birthday, Senator Daniel Webster of Massachusetts drew a similarly eloquent distinction between the freedoms of an American Republic and the ambitions of an American empire:

Other misfortunes may be borne or their effects overcome. If disastrous war should sweep our commerce from the ocean, another generation may renew it. If it exhaust our Treasury, future industry may replenish it. If it desolate and lay waste our fields, still, under a new cultivation, they will grow green again and ripen to future harvests. It were but a trifle even if the walls of yonder Capitol were to crumble, if its lofty pillars should fall, and its gorgeous decorations be all covered by the dust of the valley. All these might be rebuilt. But who shall reconstruct the fabric of demolished government? Who shall rear again the well-proportioned columns of constitutional liberty? Who shall frame together the skillful architecture which unites national sovereignty with State rights, individual security, and public prosperity? No. If these columns fall, they will be raised not again. Like the Colosseum and the

A few years prior to writing his letter to Washington, Paine had published *The Age of Reason,* the pamphlet in which he ridiculed the fiction of an established church and remarked on "the unrelenting vindictiveness with which more than half the Bible is filled." On the Continent the argument was understood as a brief for the Enlightenment, but the American congregation found Paine guilty of the crime of blasphemy. On his return from France to Baltimore in 1802, a Federalist crowd met him at the dock with jeers and cat-calls, damning him as a "drunkard" and "a brutal infidel." When he died in 1809, his body was denied burial in hallowed ground, and throughout the whole of the nineteenth century, American preachers brandished the name of "Old Tom" as a synonym for the devil.*

As true now as they were two hundred years ago, Paine's writings speak to the vanity of an American government so convinced that it is doing God's will on earth that it hears in the voices of dissent the whisperings of Satan. At few other

---

Parthenon, they will be destined to a mournful, a melancholy immortality. Bitterer tears, however, will flow over them than were ever shed over the monuments of Roman or Grecian art. For they will be the remnants of a more glorious edifice than Greece or Rome ever saw: the edifice of constitutional American liberty.

*Not that Paine has been without his admirers—Abraham Lincoln ("I never tire of reading Paine"); Walt Whitman ("amongst the best and truest of men"); Thomas A. Edison ("our greatest political thinker"). All character witnesses of some distinction, of course, but not to be trusted with money and therefore unrepresentative of what we mean by justice and what we know as freedom.

moments in its history has the country confronted so sharp a crisis of national definition; seldom has it found itself more sorely in need of citizens willing to ask rude questions. The senior managers of the Bush administration make no secret of their contempt for the rules of democratic procedure (inefficient, wrongheaded, and slow), of their distrust of the American people (indolent and immoral, undeserving of the truth), of their disdain for the United Nations and the prospect of international law (sophomoric idealisms embraced by weak nations too poor to pay for a serious air force). Better understood as utopian anarchists or radical nationalists than as prudent conservatives, they offer to the weaker nations of the earth (as well as to those of their fellow citizens whom they name as un-American) a choice similar to the one presented by the officers of the Spanish Inquisition to individuals charged with heresy—"Profess your faith in us, or we will burn you at the stake."

Suspicious of low-born historical fact, the Republican majorities in both the government and the media belong to the party of transcendence, imagining themselves as bearers of a higher truth, at odds with a world they never made, captivated by the beauty of ideological abstraction, treacherously arraigned by hideous giants and demonic apparitions instead of by the ordinary interests and desires of other human beings. They bring to Washington the certain knowledge that they can do no wrong, and they define evil as a pollutant borne on an alien wind; nothing to do with man's inward nature but something that arrives, inexplicably, from the sea, the ozone layer, or the slums. Attorney General

Ashcroft struck the preferred note of blameless virtue in his autobiography, *On My Honor,* a confession of faith in which he observes that "the verdict of history is inconsequential; the verdict of eternity is what counts." The dogma nullifies the premise of a government of laws made by men, for and with other men, framed to the contingencies of the world in time and subject to no other verdict except that of history.

When carried into the arenas of foreign policy, the belief in America's always perfect innocence supports the Bush administration's doctrine of forward deterrence and preemptive strike. The immaculate republic invariably finds itself betrayed, and because it has been betrayed, it can justify the use of criminal means to defend itself against the world's wickedness. American armies go forth into the deserts of iniquity on behalf of all mankind, in order to forestall any upstart challenge to America's unblemished moral sovereignty. The imperialist line of thought was well entrenched in Washington long before the terrorist onslaught of September 11, 2001. In 1993 the Pentagon released a policy paper, *Defense Strategy for the 1990s,* that had been drafted two years earlier by Dick Cheney, Colin Powell, and Paul Wolfowitz. The three authors were then serving as senior counselors in the administration of the elder President Bush; the document acknowledges and accepts America's mission to rule the world, clearly setting forth the theory of domination subsequently incorporated into what became known, in the autumn of 2002, as the Bush Doctrine.

More than once during the decade of the 1990s I attended a National Security Conference in Washington at which the senior statesmen seated on the dais could be counted on to say—always with a note of regret, of course, and wishing they didn't have to be so blunt—that America wasn't likely to come to its senses unless or until something really awful happened. The citizenry was drifting into moral relativism and cultural decline, the schools all but fully submerged in the swamp of materialism, and somehow the country needed to be reawakened to the fact that the world was a far more dangerous place than had been dreamed of in the philosophy of Jerry Seinfeld or the World Wildlife Fund.

Because the gentlemen on the dais had served the administrations of Presidents Ronald Reagan and George H. W. Bush as secretaries of defense or state, sometimes as chiefs of naval operations or directors of the Central Intelligence Agency, their geopolitics were understood to bear the stamps of selfless patriotism. Invariably their remarks were received with approving murmurs of wise assent, which wasn't surprising because the meetings invariably had been called to order by one or another of the neoconservative think tanks dedicated to the cause of an assertive American foreign policy. The high-end intellectuals in the room (sometimes Richard Perle, often William Bennett accompanied by a smirk of columnists from the *Weekly Standard*) never tired of telling the travelers from New York (over coffee between the morning's first and second power points; while investigating the poached salmon before the luncheon speech) that the ideas of government made to the measure of a provincial democratic republic (America in 1941) could no longer accommodate the interests of a global nation-state that deserved to wear the crown and name of empire (America, circa 1995).

It wasn't that anybody had intended so impressive a metamorphosis, but how could it be otherwise? The Russians had lost the cold war, their weapons gone to rust, their economy in ruins, and the statues of V. I. Lenin reduced to a rubble of broken stones. From the Chinese not even Henry Kissinger expected anything but a supply of cheap labor for another thirty years. If not America, "the world's only surviving superpower," who else could lift the imperial burden once carried on the back of Rome? Now that history was at an end, the American way was the only way, and where else except in Washington to kiss the kindly hand of power?*

John Quincy Adams appreciated the weight and cost of the imperial burden as long ago as 1821, when, as secretary of state, he opposed the sending of the U.S. Navy to overthrow

---

*Charles Krauthammer, a columnist for the *Washington Post* and a leading proponent of the Pax Americana, gave voice to the sentiment in *Time* magazine in March 2001, six months before the destruction of the World Trade Center: "America is no mere international citizen. It is the dominant power in the world, more dominant than any since Rome. Accordingly, America is in a position to reshape norms, alter expectations and create new realities. How? By unapologetic and implacable demonstrations of will."

The dream of empire is not unique to Republicans. In 1998, while serving as secretary of state in the Clinton administration, Madeleine Albright asserted America's right to use unilateral force against Saddam Hussein because "we are America. We are the indispensable nation. We stand tall. We see further into the future."

Spain's colonial viceroys in Venezuela and Peru. "America," he said, "goes not abroad, in search of monsters to destroy." Were the country to embark on such a foolish adventure,

> she would involve herself beyond the power of extrica-
> tion, in all the wars of interest and intrigue, of individual
> avarice, envy, and ambition, which assume the colors and
> usurp the standard of freedom. The fundamental maxims
> of her policy would insensibly change from *liberty* to
> *force....* She might become the dictatress of the world.
> She would no longer be the ruler of her own spirit.

The Bush administration equates the American spirit with force, not with liberty, and it looks for monsters to destroy at every point of the moral and geopolitical compass. Unable to erect a secure perimeter around the entire landscape of a free society by posting agents at checkpoints both temporal and spiritual, the government bureaus of public safety solve the technical problems by seeing to it that the society becomes less free. They make a good deal of brave noise about their great and noble projects of regime change in Afghanistan and Iraq, but on the evidence of the last two years they have been doing their most effective work in the United States. If not as a concerted effort to restrict the liberties of the American people, how else does one describe the Republican agenda now in motion in the nation's capital? The administration assumes the colors and usurps the standard of freedom to mobilize not the defense of the American citizenry against a foreign enemy but the protection of the American plutocracy from the American democracy. It has been supported in the enterprise by a servile Congress that bows to the constituencies of fear and nationalist sentiment and approves the requested legislation as promptly as if it had been called on to save a sinking ship with the rapid slamming of steel doors. In every instance, and no matter what the issue immediately at hand, the purpose is the same— more laws limiting the freedom of individuals, fewer laws restraining the freedoms of property:

1. the systematic transfer of the nation's wealth from the union of the poor to the confederacy of the rich, the intention made plain in the various tax bills that reduce or eliminate the burdens on unearned income;

2. the easing of environmental regulations on the energy industries in New England, and the opening of the national forests in the Pacific Northwest and the Arctic National Wildlife Refuge to further expropriation by the oil, gas, mining, and timber industries;

3. the persistent issuing of health insurance regulations intended to subvert and eventually overturn the 1973 Supreme Court ruling *Roe* v. *Wade,* which recognized a woman's freedom to decide whether or not she will give birth to a child;

4. the reinforcing of the monopolies held by the big media syndicates on the country's systems of communication;

5. the equipping of banks and credit card agencies with the privilege to sell to the highest bidders any and all of the personal data acquired from their customers;

6. a series of proposals meant to reduce the nation's health care costs by denying medical services to people too poor to pay for the upkeep of the insurance companies;

7. the putting in place of "tort reforms" that make it more difficult for state and federal courts to entertain class-action lawsuits on behalf of citizens harmed by corporate swindling or malfeasance;

8. the broad expansion of the government's police powers under the USA PATRIOT and Homeland Security Acts, the Justice Department reserving to itself the right to decide who is and who is not an un-American; and

9. the nomination to the federal appeals courts of judges apt to find legal precedents in the pages of the Bible rather than in the articles of the Constitution.

The ease with which the legislative measures attract non-partisan majorities bespeaks a politically demobilized society and reflects the grotesque maldistribution of wealth that over the last thirty years has transferred 80 percent of the country's net worth to 10 percent of the citizenry. Whether Republican or Democrat, the tribunes of the people dance to the tune of the same big but nervous money, their differences of opinion of as little consequence as the choice between the grilled and potted shrimp. Bought at auction as a collection of lapel pins (some in the shape of elephants, others in the shape of donkeys), they represent the comforts of the frightened rich and speak to the interests of a selfish oligarchy anxious to preserve its privileges in the impregnable vaults of military empire. On the floor of Congress, as in the chambers of the Supreme Court and the executive suites of the White House and the Pentagon, the absence of the will and spirit of what was once a democratic republic bears out John Kenneth Galbraith's observation that "the deepest instinct of the affluent, whether in America, Germany, or Argentina, is to believe that what's good for them is what's good for the country." People supported by incomes of $10 million or $15 million a year not only enjoy a style of living unavailable to those with incomes of $50,000 or even $150,000 a year, they also acquire different habits of mind— they are reluctant to think for themselves, afraid of the future, careful to expatriate their profits in offshore tax havens, disinclined to trust a new hairdresser or a new idea, grateful for the security of gated residential protectorates, reassured by reactionary political theorists who say that history is at an end and that if events should threaten to prove otherwise (angry mobs throwing stones in third-world slums), America will send an army to exterminate the brutes. Not an inspiring set of attitudes, but representative of the social class that owns our news media, staffs the government, and pays for our elections.

Neither the media nor the universities have yet come up with an adequate name or phrase for the American ruling class. The United States doesn't possess "an establishment" in the British sense of the word; "plutocracy" is too vague, and "upper class" implies a veneer of manners that exists only in the style section of the *Washington Post*. Borrowed from Roman usage, the term "equestrian class" comprises all those who can afford to ride rather than walk and who can buy the baubles that constitute the emblems of social prominence. As with the ancient Romans, the rank is for sale.*

President Bush pledged allegiance to what have become the American house rules when, on arriving in Washington in the winter of 2001, he let it be known that he intended to

---

*The upper servants of the status quo don't choose to acknowledge the prerogatives of privilege that we meet every day in the street, and they flood the country's editorial markets with reassuring cant about the country's lack of class consciousness. The words to the wise invariably repeat the lesson taught by Norman Rockwell, Walt Disney, and the editors of the *Wall Street Journal*. A few liberties having been taken with the paraphrase, the standard text reads as follows:

Being American and therefore blessed at birth with the gene of egalitarianism, we don't envy people richer than ourselves; nor do we labor in the shadow of the false class distinctions that still cloud the mind of Old Europe. If a CEO earns five hundred times as much money as one of his secretaries or assembly-line workers ($15 million as opposed to $30,000 per annum), it doesn't mean that the CEO is a selfish thug. The suspicion is invidious and French. The nice man owes his good fortune to hard work and his belief in God. We don't begrudge him his opulent lifestyle (too snooty, not enough time for his neighbors, his children, or his golf swing) because we know that soon, probably sooner than anyone thinks, we ourselves will become rich. In the meantime, while waiting for the report from the assay office or the coroner, we are expectant capitalists, devoid of resentment, happy to be living in a land of great abundance and unlimited opportunity. We are Americans, bless our hearts, just folks who would rather be shopping at Wal-

run the government as if it were a business. Three years later it comes as no surprise that the ten-year federal budget projection has changed from a $5.6 trillion surplus to a $4 trillion deficit, or that our splendid little war in Iraq turns out to have been sold to the American public in the manner of a well-promoted but fraudulent stock offering. The man has been true to his word, the corporation of which he deems himself chairman and chief executive officer not unlike the ones formerly owned and operated by his friends and fundraisers at Enron and Arthur Andersen. The administration's economic and military schemes rely on budget analysts who reconfigure debt as credit, on auditors at the intelligence agencies who rig their balance sheets with sham transactions (for African uranium), false data (establishing Saddam Hussein's connection to Al Qaeda), offshore special-purpose entities (to contain the otherwise invisible weapons of mass destruction).

Because the Bush administration's modus operandi resembles that of a corrupt monopoly (publicly owned but privately managed), much of its domestic and foreign policy can be understood in terms of the hidden surcharge and the dishonest annual report. "Fraud" is another word for "free-

---

Mart than at one of those fancy stores on Madison Avenue or Rodeo Drive, and anybody who wants to talk to us about class conflict or Karl Marx better damned well know that we don't hold with the notion of a society that looks like some sort of English layer cake. The American oligarchy doesn't prey on the American democracy, because in America we have no such thing as an oligarchy. Perish the thought!

dom," "to make a killing" the highest form of patriotism or praise. Mark up the price of the American military occupation of Iraq from $2 billion to $4 billion a month, or guide WorldCom into the desert of a $9 billion accounting error, and whether it is Donald Rumsfeld explaining the arithmetic to Tim Russert, or Bernard Ebbers, the president of World-Com, answering the questions of a judge, the story follows a by-now-familiar script—a once-trusted institution becomes entangled in the nets of perjury and graft, assets worth $100 million depart for points unknown, the stock price falls from ninety-five dollars to thirty cents a share, the company's pensioners are hounded into penury. The high-end executives meanwhile cash their stock options at the best possible price, reward their own grand and petty larcenies with severance payments in amounts upward of $30 million, retain the apartment in Paris and the bank account in Zurich, go off to Colorado with the golf clubs and the skis. Transfer the procedure from the private to the public sector and the government fattens the defense budget by sending the soldiers and the tanks out to pasture in Iraq, clears the Pentagon's inventory of weapons no longer stylish, and distributes the construction contracts to any Texas friend of liberty willing to lend a hand with the oil derricks around Baghdad and the balloons at next year's Republican nominating convention.*

---

*Up front and unapologetic about its plundering of the American commonwealth on behalf of its corporate sponsors and accomplices, the Bush administration follows a practice well established by both its near and its distant predecessors. The raids on the federal treasury encouraged by the Reagan administration took

It wasn't as if the Bush administration failed to serve notice of its character and intentions. During the forty days and forty nights when the president's accession to the White House still hinged on the counting of the vote in Florida, the television footage from Washington and Palm Beach supplied hourly proofs of what we have come to mean by the phrases "rule of law," "democratic self-government," and "free and fair elections." I didn't follow all the lines of all the legal maneuvers, but I remember being struck by the poison-

---

place under the cover of a darkness represented as an ideological awakening. Deregulation was the watchword for the transfer of wealth from the public to the private sector, the $500 billion savings-and-loan swindle an exemplary proof of what could be done with the theory that big government (by definition wasteful and incompetent) must be dismembered and sold for scrap to the entrepreneurs in our midst (by definition innovative and efficient) who know how to privatize profit while socializing the risk and cost. Diligently applied by a succession of industrious thieves over the last twenty-five years, the theory has resulted in the wreckage of the airline industry, the degradation of the environment, the monopolies' strangling the wit and sense out of the news media, the Enron and WorldCom debacles, and most recently the award of no-bid contracts to the Bechtel Corporation (in the amount of $2.8 billion) and to Halliburton ($6.4 billion) for the reconstruction of Iraq.

The looting is traditional, the rule of capture as firmly rooted in the country's history as the belief in angels. Epitomized in the mottoes "Boom and bust," "Settle and sell," "Get in, get rich, get out," the winning of the nineteenth-century American West was a public works project paid for with federal subsidies. By 1850 everybody traveling west of the Mississippi understood that the new line of the country was ripe with four primary resources—land, minerals, timber, and government contracts—and that of these, by far the richest was the government contract. The trick was to know the right people in Washington, in the state capital, around the county courthouse.

ous language dribbling out of the mouths of people who as recently as the preceding summer had been talking about restoring "civility to the American political discourse." The Republicans never tired of accusing the Democrats of trying to steal the election ("chad molesters," "commanders in thief"), but it was their own behavior that more nearly resembled that of Mafia bagmen hurrying to get the votes across the border and out of state before somebody searched their luggage. A court that ruled in favor of George W. Bush was a court deserving of compliance and respect; a court that ruled otherwise was a treasonous court, renegade and corrupt. Citizens allied with the prima facie righteousness of the Republican cause deserved the name of patriot; Democrats were partisan hacks, by definition crooked and self-serving, slum-dwelling perps, accustomed to stealing elections and cars.*

---

*The voices of Republican alarm in the print and television media upgraded their rhetoric to the pitch of near hysteria. The *Wall Street Journal*'s lead editorial accused the Democrats of attempting a "coup d'état." The columnists elsewhere on the page likened Al Gore to Adolf Hitler and Al Capone; every Democratic legal argument was "preposterous" or "illegitimate," every filing of a motion on Mr. Gore's behalf "an unfolding miscarriage of justice." The *National Review* displayed the fear and loathing of a columnist by the name of Mark Steyn. Puzzled and disturbed by the unexpectedly large numbers of voters who had preferred the Democratic candidate, Steyn asked himself the question, "Who *are* these people?" and fortunately discovered, much to his relief, that most of them were misfits, criminals, and foreigners—"aliens Al Gore strong-armed the INS into hustling through the naturalization process without background checks," also the friends of Al Sharpton and Alec Baldwin, senile pensioners rounded up from nursing homes, "Gay scout leaders," "partial abortion fetishists," and "the Palm Beach chapter of Jews for Buchanan."

On the evening of November 21, James A. Baker III, secretary of state in the administration of George H. W. Bush,
on temporary loan to George W. Bush's election campaign,
angrily informed a press conference in Tallahassee that the
Florida Supreme Court committed what he construed to be
the crime of lèse-majesté, and watching him read his statement to the cameras I understood that he conceived the law
as a nuisance, an idiot tangle of "legalistic language," superfluous and tiresome, an insult in the mouths of people too
poor or too weak to buy what they wished or do as they
pleased. The expression in Baker's face—pinched, vengeful,
and mean—vouched for the great oligarchic truth summed
up in the phrase "Unless we win, it's illegal," and it wasn't
hard to guess that to Mr. Baker and the custodians of the Republican conscience, the laws were forms of crowd control,
the power of government not that of a creative agency or a
constructive force but the power to punish and restrict, the
power of the customs official, the police sergeant, the traffic
judge, and the Eighty-second Airborne Division.*

The same ugly turn of mind governed the planning and

---

*William Rehnquist, chief justice of the Supreme Court, served as a government
enforcer during the Nixon administration. Breveted to the Justice Department in
1969, he approved the plan drawn up by Tom Houston, a White House aide, that
commissioned the American military to set up prison camps for the incarcera-
tion of hundreds of thousands of opponents to the Vietnam War. Testifying before a Senate committee in 1971, Rehnquist said that it was legal, under the
president's authority, to send the army to suppress rebellions and enforce the
laws. In 1998 he published a book, *All the Laws but One,* in which he argued that
in time of war, civil liberties were not to be too carefully protected.

production of a war in Iraq intended to serve not only as a
showcase for the Pentagon's new and exciting inventory of
terrible weapons but also as a test market for a reconfigured
American political idea matched to Benito Mussolini's definition of fascism, "which should more properly be called
corporatism, since it is the merger of state and corporate
power." Envisioning a slum clearance project for the whole
of the Islamic Middle East, Iraq the first in a series of model
satrapies soon to be erected in Syria, Iran, Libya, Egypt, and
Saudi Arabia, the would-be proconsuls of the Bush administration further assume the absence of strenuous objection on
the part of an American public and an American news media
content to drift from news cycle to news cycle in a state of
political somnambulism not much different from their own.

The supposition isn't entirely wrong. The Bush administration owes its existence to our apathy and sloth. The successful
operation of a democracy relies on acts of self-government
by no means easy to perform, and for the last twenty years
we have been unwilling to do the work. Our prosperity has
financed the habit of indolence. Choosing to believe that the
public good comes to us at the discretion of private wealth,
we don't bother to vote, don't read through the list of budget
appropriations, accept the opinions advertised on prime-
time television by talk-show hosts stamped with the labels of
celebrity. We leave the small print for the lawyers to clean and
maybe press, and in place of an energetic politics we get by
with nostalgic sentiment and the public-spirited postcards

sent by PBS—liberty a trust fund and America the land in which the money never dies. If we have allowed the American political argument to degenerate into mindless catch-phrase and fifteen-minute sound bite, how can we not expect our government to speak the same language, to tell the easy and patriotic lie, and whenever it doesn't know what else to do, to arrest mysterious strangers and bomb Baghdad?

Dependent on the carelessness of an electorate in a hurry to get to the tennis court or the beach, the Bush administration relies on the lessons of obedience taught to a once-free people during the second half of a century defined as America's own. Begin the narrative almost anywhere in the late 1940s or early 1950s—with the National Security Act of 1947, the hearings before the House Un-American Activities Committee in 1951, the composition of the Hollywood black-list or Senator Joe McCarthy's search for Marxists marching in the Rose Bowl Parade—and even an inattentive historian can see the quick and eager smiles of loyal agreement coming to be preferred to the hesitant professions of an awkward or unwelcome truth. I'm old enough to remember public speeches unfettered by the dogma of political correctness, a time when it was possible to apply for a job without submitting a blood or urine test, when people construed their freedoms as a constitutional birthright, not as favors bestowed by a sometimes benevolent bureaucracy. I also can remember the days when people weren't afraid of tobacco, sexual intercourse, and unsaturated fats; when irony was understood and money wasn't sacred, when even men in uniform could be trusted to get the joke.

The once-familiar atmospheres of liberty—wisecracking and open-ended, tolerant, unkempt, spacious, and democratic—didn't serve the purposes of the cold war with the Russians, and the easygoing, provincial republic of fifty years ago gradually has assumed the character of a world-encircling nation-state, borrowing from its enemies (first the Communist politburo, now the terrorist jihad) the practice of restricting the freedom of its own citizens in the interest of what the increasingly autocratic governments in Washington proclaim to be the "national security." Add to the constant threat of nuclear extinction the sum of wiretaps infiltrated into the American consciousness across the span of three generations, and it's no wonder that by the late 1990s, even in the midst of the reassuring prosperity allied with a buoyant stock market and well before the destruction of the World Trade Center, the public opinion polls found a clear majority willing to give up a generous percentage of their essential liberty in return for safer streets, secure suburbs, well-lighted parking garages, and risk-free cocktail waitresses.

The shock of September 11, 2001, quickened the pace of the retreat into the shelters of harmless speech and heavy law enforcement. Measuring the general level of submissiveness by my own encounters with the habits of self-censorship and the niceties of social hygiene, I find acquaintances reluctant to remark on the brutality of the Israeli army for fear of being thought anti-Semitic, public scolds who damn me as a terrorist for smoking a cigarette in Central Park, college students so worried about the grooming of their résumés that they avoid rock concerts on the off chance that their faces might show up in a police department videotape. It's not hard to argue that America's winning of the war on terror must result in the loss of what John Quincy Adams named as its ruling spirit. In place of the reckless and independent-minded individual once thought to embody the national stereotype (descendant of Davy Crockett and Daniel Boone, child of nature, hard-drinking, and unorthodox), we now have a quorum of anxious careerists, psalm-singing and well behaved, happy to oblige, eager to please, trained to hold up their hands and empty their pockets when passing through airport security or entering city hall.

In concert with the government's increasingly swell-headed pretensions to imperial grandeur over the last twenty years, the increasingly delicate etiquette of political correctness has cleansed the news media of strong language and imperfect hair, inoculated college seminars against the infection of subversive adjectives, and removed from grammar schools the presence of offending nouns. Among the topics ruled inadmissible on its roster of searching essay questions, the Princeton Review now lists, in no particular order, war, drugs, sex, alcohol, tobacco, junk food, socioeconomic advantages, divorce, religion, Halloween, and anything "disrespectful" or "demeaning." A further clarification, published in the summer of 2003, Diane Ravitch's book *The Language Police,* takes note of the same fastidiousness governing the assembly of high school textbooks, and as examples of the words and images deleted in the interest of a risk-free intellectual environment she mentions Mickey Mouse and Stuart Little (both rodents and therefore suggestive of rats in slums), depictions of a mother cooking dinner for her children (gender stereo-type), dinosaurs (their presence lending credibility to the the-ory of evolution), owls (in some cultures associated with death). The committees buying the freshly laundered lesson plans seek "multidimensional companionship" with the cen-sors on the Christian right, who compose pictures of a non-existent past, and the censors on the academic left, who compose pictures of a nonexistent future. The handsomely il-lustrated workbooks aspire to the serenity of advertisements for cosmetics or detergents, the words deserving of the same labels, "risk-averse," "salt-free," "baby-soft."

Conceived in the universities in the early 1980s, the doc-trine of political correctness was meant to empower what was then perceived as the disenfranchised left—women, gays, blacks, Latinos, environmentalists, any and all victims of circumstance. The speaking in euphemisms, like the speaking in Pentecostal tongues, supposedly conferred on the devotees the mandate of heaven. Teach people to talk sweetly to one another, divide the curriculum into communi-ties of uplifting sentiment (sexual and cultural as well as racial and socioeconomic), and then surely, in the fullness of time and after many repetitions of the magic words, they will learn to behave properly, to abandon the joys of date rape and haul down their Confederate flags, to come to see and know that the true path to political happiness is found not with a compass or an argument but with a well-thumbed the-saurus.

The society's corporate managers needed twenty years to

appreciate the full value of the gift they had been given. The events of September 11, 2001, placed the doctrine of safe speech in a truer light and a clearer perspective. The distortions of language formerly regarded as the enemy of free expression stood revealed as the friend of Operation Iraqi Freedom. With only slight adjustments in emphasis, the rinsed and blow-dried vocabulary proved better suited to the empowering of the state than to the protection of individuals against attacks on their emotional well-being.

At the universities nobody knew how to change women into men or black people into white people, but the least that anybody could do was to pretend otherwise. It wasn't appropriate to observe that the progenitors of Western civilization were for the most part European, male and white; it wasn't appropriate to say that women tend not to be drawn to the study of mathematics or drafted into the secondary of the Chicago Bears.

Deployed in the theaters of military operation, the polite uses of language allow the Pentagon spokespersons to conduct their briefings in the manner of English professors teaching classes in semantics. Nobody knows how to fight wars without killing people, but the least they can do is to pretend otherwise. When the American commanders in Iraq talk about "appropriate levels of combat power," none of the reporters attending the class inquires about the chance of casualties—military, civilian, or collateral. To do so would be "inappropriate" for the same reason that the Bush administration deems it "inappropriate" to permit photographs of the flag-draped coffins offloaded on the ramps of Dover Air Force Base.

Let it once be established that prejudice is an evil with a thousand faces and as many names (the bias against fat people or Yorkshire terriers as small-minded and contemptible as the bias against black people or parakeets), and there's no end of the services that the word can be made to perform. The intelligentsia on the Republican right picked up on the possibilities during the first term of the Clinton administration, developing the theory of rich white men as an oppressed minority suffering under the lash of federal tax policy and Michael Moore's jokes. The election of George Bush brought them out of the closet, teaching them to recognize a form of ethnic identity too long submerged by an alien culture insensitive to the humiliation of a Wednesday without oysters or a Sunday without polo.*

The ritual cleansings of the language conform to the idea that politics, by definition filthy, doesn't matter, which is the lie that has been sold by the merchants of the country's upscale socioeconomic opinion in all the better stores and newspapers ever since Ronald Reagan first opened his window on

---

*The enemies of the inheritance tax have found in Grover Norquist, president of Americans for Tax Reform, their own Martin Luther King Jr., leading them out of darkness, striking off their chains. Not a man afraid to speak out against social injustice, Norquist entered the plea of racism on October 2, in a conversation with Terry Gross on the National Public Radio program *Fresh Air*. Comparing the cadre of wealthy Americans to the victims of the Holocaust, Norquist said:

the White House lawn to discover that once again it was "morning in America." Of what consequence the tiresome questions of law and public policy when compared with the wonders of Microsoft and the miracle of the markets for California telecommunications technology and Arizona real estate? The country's immense prosperity during the decades of the 1980s and 1990s (the nation's household assets up from $6.5 trillion to $35 trillion, the GDP up from $4.9 trillion to $9.2 trillion) lent credence to the theory of a future that could be bought instead of earned. History was mercifully at an end, the art of politics (embarrassingly human and therefore corrupt) subordinate to the science of economics (reassuringly abstract and therefore perfect). The financial markets (light unto the nations, answer to everybody's prayers) made all the decisions of any consequence or size; politicians handed around the party hats and hired the mariachi band. The presumptions of wealth and ease made possible Bill Clinton's extended run on the Washington stage and provided the background music for the presidential election of 2000, the two candidates presenting themselves as harmless ornamental figures bearing well-bred names, both of them valuable objects certain to go with the furniture in

---

The morality that says it's okay to do something to a group because they're a small percentage of the population is the morality that says the Holocaust is okay because they didn't target everybody, just a small percentage. . . . Arguing that it's okay to loot some group because it's them, or kill some group because it's them, and because it's a small number—that has no place in a democratic society.

the dining room or the den, both available from the Hor-
chow catalog.

The attitude doesn't match the color scheme of the killing
in Iraq. If we took more of an interest in the making of a
foreign policy meant to protect the profits of the American
oligarchy rather than the safety of the American democracy,
maybe we would know why, when bringing the lamp of liberty to the darker places of the earth, the United States invariably chooses for its allies the despots who operate their
countries on the model of a prison or a jail.

Although good with slogans, the makers of American
foreign policy don't have much talent for fostering the construction of exemplary democracies; drawn to dictators
whom we hire to represent our freedom-loving commercial
interests (Ngo Dinh Diem, the Shah of Shahs, Anastasio So-
moza, Nguyen Van Thieu, Ferdinand Marcos, Jonas Savimbi,
Manuel Noriega, Saddam Hussein, King Fahd, Mobuto Sese
Seko), we pretend that our new ally stands as a pillar of
democracy in one or another of the world's poorer latitudes,
and for however many years the arrangement lasts we send
F-16s and messages of humanitarian concern. But then
something goes amiss with the band music or the tin mines;
the despot's palace guard doesn't know how to fire the ma-
chine guns, or fires them at the wrong people, and the prime
minister's brother appropriates the traffic in cocaine. We decide that our virtue has been compromised, or that we no
longer can afford the cost of the parliament, and we leave in
a helicopter from the roof of the nearest embassy.

If we mean to project abroad the force and image of a

democratic *res publica* made glorious by the death of American teenagers and Muslim holy men, we also might want to consider taking better care of our own domestic commonwealth. For the last twenty years we've let fall into disrepair nearly all of the public infrastructure—roads, water systems, schools, power plants, bridges, hospitals, broadcast frequencies—that provides the country with the foundation of its common enterprise.

Forty years ago in the United States the word "public" served as a synonym for selfless dedication to the common good (public servant, public health, public interest) and the word "private" carried with it the suggestion of selfish greed (private interest, private bank, private railroad car). Two generations of sustained economic prosperity have reversed the political usages of the words. "Public" connotes waste, poverty, incompetence, and fraud; "private" connotes honesty, intelligence, efficiency, and noble purpose. Ballparks and convention centers bear the names of telephone and airline companies; athletes wear the insignia of their sponsors; the Boston subway system offers to sell the naming rights to four of its busiest and most historic stations, among them Back Bay and Downtown Crossing, to any business enterprise willing to pay an annual fee somewhere in the vicinity of $2 million. New York City rents its uniformed police officers (twenty-seven dollars an hour plus handling charges) to any uptown optimate seeking to provide a private dance or dinner party with an atmosphere of stately and reassuring calm. The officers come complete with bulletproof vests and the powers of arrest; the client pays for the liability insurance that covers the cost of lawsuits arising from complaints about the deployment of excessive force.

The privatization of the nation's public resources has enriched the investors fortunate enough to profit from the changes of venue, but at what cost to the state of our general well-being? By discounting what the brokers classify as "nonmarket values," we downgrade our faith in the republic from the strength of a conviction to the weakness of a sentiment, and we're left with a body politic defined not as the union of its collective energies and hopes but as an aggregate of loosely affiliated interests (ethnic, regional, commercial, sexual), each armed with its own manifesto, loyal to its own agenda, secure in the compound of its own jargon—democracy understood as a fancy Greek name for the American Express card, the government seen as a Florida resort hotel, its assortment of goods and services deserving of respect in the exact degree to which it satisfies the whims of its patrons and meets the expectations of comfort and style at both the discount and holiday rates.

As was demonstrated by the events of September 11, the laissez-faire theories of government do us an injustice. They don't speak to the best of our character; neither do they express the cherished ideal embodied in the history of a courageous people. What joins Americans one to another is not a common nationality, race, or ancestry but their voluntary pledge to a shared work of both the moral and the political imagination. The love of country follows from the love of its freedoms, not from pride in its armies or its fleets. Understood as useful and well-made instruments meant to support the liberties of the people (tools on the order of a plow, an ax, or a surveyor's plumb line), the institutions of democratic government provide the premise for a narrative rather than the design for a monument or the plans for an invasion.

The barbarism in Washington doesn't dress itself in the costumes of Al Qaeda; it wears instead the smooth-shaven smile of a Senate resolution sold to the highest bidder, and if we are to account for, and possibly correct, the country's reversals of fortune over the last two years, we might begin by remembering that politics are the means with which we make our freedom. The shaping of a decent American future presupposes an argument between time past and time present, between the inertia implicit in the weight of things-as-they-are and the energy inherent in the hope of things-as-they-might-become. The supporters of the status quo invariably command the popular majority; theirs is the party of the Disney Company and the Bush administration, putting out more flags, enlarging the radius of the secure perimeter, distributing the pillows of cant. They speak in the voices of Tom Brokaw and *Time* magazine—we know best; maybe two or three years from now, when all the terrorists have been rounded up and the Trade Center towers replaced with a golden statue of Mammon, the time will come to talk of politics. In the meanwhile, my children, while waiting for that far-off happy day, be patient, follow directions, submit to the surveillance, look at the nice pictures brought to you by the Pentagon, know that your rulers are wise.

The dissenting spirit stands with the party of things-as-they-might-become, acknowledging the truth of Alfred North Whitehead's observation that it is the business of the future to be dangerous—not because the future is perverse or unaffiliated with the Republican Party but because it doesn't know how to be anything else. Democracy allies itself with change and proceeds from the assumption that nobody knows enough, that nothing is final, that the old order (whether of men or institutions) will be dragged offstage when its prescriptions no longer fit the facts. The freedoms of expression present democratic societies with the unwelcome news that they are in trouble, but because all societies, like most individuals, are always in some kind of trouble, the news doesn't drive them onto the reefs of destruction. They die instead from the fear of thought and the paralysis that accompanies the wish to believe that only the wicked perish. Voiced in the first person singular and synonymous with the courage of mind that Frederick Lewis Allen, a former editor of *Harper's Magazine,* once described as "unorganized, unrecognized, unorthodox, and unterrified," dissent is what rescues democracy from a quiet death behind closed doors.

Whether we like it or not, the argument now going forward in the United States is the same argument that put an end to the Roman and Weimar Republics, built the scaffolds of the Spanish Inquisition, gave rise to the American Revolution. If we fail to engage it, we do so at our peril. It is not the law that takes freedom from us but the laziness of our own minds, the unwillingness to think for ourselves and so resign, even momentarily, from the herd. Dostoyevsky put the proposition in the voice of the grand inquisitor, who understood that the power of the Catholic Church rested on the reliably human wish to remain a slave, to prefer the comforts of magic, mystery, and authority, whenever possible to check into the nearest cage. Nobody ever said that democratic government was easy, which is why, during the twenty years between the last century's two world wars, it failed and was abandoned by the people of Italy, Turkey, Portugal, Spain, Bulgaria, Greece, Romania, Yugoslavia, Hungary, Albania, Poland, Estonia, Latvia, Lithuania, Austria, and Germany.

The failure in Germany is the one that comes most readily to mind when I read in the papers that President Bush reserves to himself the right to declare any American citizen an "enemy combatant," or, when talking with people in New York about the Justice Department's newly acquired weapons of mass investigation, I listen to them compare intrusive intelligence gathering to state-of-the-art weather forecasting—a routine and necessary precaution, annoying and possibly unconstitutional but entirely appropriate in time of trouble. I think of the German misfortune because I'm familiar with much of the testimony of the witnesses who recorded it, and I remember not only the writing of William Shirer, Christopher Isherwood, and Thomas Mann, but also Milton Mayer's *They Thought They Were Free: The Germans 1933–1945*. Mayer published the book ten years after the collapse of Hitler's Third Reich, assigning its most acute observations to "a colleague of mine, a philologist," who describes the loss of

freedom as so slow a descent into the maelstrom that it is almost imperceptible:

> What happened here was the gradual habituation of the
> people, little by little, to being governed by surprise; to re-
> ceiving decisions deliberated in secret, to believing that
> the situation was so complicated that the government had
> to act on information which the people could not under-
> stand, or so dangerous that, even if the people could un-
> derstand it, it could not be released because of national
> security. . . . I do not speak of your "little men," your
> baker and so on; I speak of my colleagues and myself,
> learned men, mind you. Most of us did not want to think
> about fundamental things and never had. There was no
> need to. Nazism gave us some dreadful, fundamental
> things to think about—we were decent people—and kept
> us so busy with continuous changes and "crises" and so
> fascinated, yes, fascinated, by the machinations of the
> "national enemies," without and within, that we had no
> time to think about those dreadful things that were grow-
> ing, little by little, all around us. Unconsciously, I suppose,
> we were grateful. Who wants to think?*

---

*Mayer's book deserves quotation at more length, if for no other reason than to
disturb the complacence of people who say, smilingly, and as if from a great
height, "Yes, but that was then, and this is now, and besides, it can't happen here."
It happened in Greece; it happened in Rome; it can happen aboard the starship
Enterprise. At the risk of trying the reader's patience, again Mayer:

Jefferson believed that the tree of liberty needed to be nourished every now and then with the blood of revolution. I don't know whether the time has come again to storm the palace and seize the radio station, but the government now in Washington doesn't meet the specifications of the one envisioned in the Declaration of Independence. The signers of the Declaration staked their lives, their fortunes, and their sacred honor on the proposition that when government becomes oppressively corrupt, it is not only the right but also the duty of the people to revolt. So it was said and believed in Philadelphia in 1776; so it can be said and believed nearly anywhere in the United States in 2004. We have a government in Washington that doesn't defend the liberty of the American people, steals from the poor to feed the rich, finds its wealth and happiness in the waging of ceaseless war. Where else do we turn except to politics, and how else do our politics get made if not with the voices of dissent? Rightly understood, democracy is an uproar, and if we mean to engage the argument about the course of the American future,

---

To live in this process is absolutely not to be able to notice it—please try to believe me—unless one has a much greater degree of political awareness, acuity, than most of us had ever had occasion to develop. Each step was so small, so inconsequential, so well explained or, on occasion, "regretted," that, unless one were detached from the whole process from the beginning, unless one understood what the whole thing was in principle, what all these "little measures" that no "patriotic German" could resent must some day lead to, one no more saw it developing from day to day than a farmer in his field sees the corn growing. One day it is over his head.

let us hope that it proves to be loud, disorderly, bitter, and fierce.*

This year's presidential election offers the American people a choice between the hardships of self-rule and the comforts of autocracy, and if it's fair to judge by the combativeness showing up in the letters to the editor of *Harper's Magazine* (also on the letters columns of the *New York Times,* the *Washington Post,* and sometimes the *Wall Street Journal*), the electorate is by no means as dumb or as uninterested as dreamed of in the philosophy of Karl Rove. I'm struck by the force of the language rising to counter what a woman in Oceanside, California, describes as "this grinning pestilence of a government in Washington." Addressing every topic on the list of the country's political misfortunes—the tragic and farcical attempt at military empire in Iraq, the suddenly "swollen tumor" of a federal debt likely to beggar the next generation of our own citizens, the "criminal assault" on our civil liberties conducted by an attorney general who believes that God wrote the Constitution and the Bill of Rights—the correspondents hold to the premise on which the country

---

*The idea as well as the practice of democracy is so foreign to most of the country's expensive journalists that on the night when the votes were being counted in Florida during the last presidential election, the anchorpersons in the broadcast booths showed a marked resemblance to aquarium fish. Their mouths were opening and closing; they were floating around in their state-of-the-art habitats, the red-and-blue maps as colorful as tiny coral reefs, but when they peered into the glass wall of the camera, it was as if they were wondering what had happened to the Caribbean Sea. Astonishingly, and for the first time in twelve months, the

was founded and join with James Madison in the assumption that whereas "in Europe charters of liberty had been granted by power," America has set the example of "charters of power granted by liberty." The letters prove a point opposite to the one that their authors sometimes intend, the humor and energy of the prose giving the lie to the professions of cynicism and despair.

So also do the manifestations of dissent breaking through the ropelines of consensus everywhere else in the society—at political rallies for the season's Democratic presidential candidates, in messages posted on the Internet, in the sales figures reported for Gore Vidal's *Inventing a Nation* and Michael Moore's *Dude, Where's My Country?*, in newspaper advertisements placed by the American Civil Liberties Union and moveon.org, and even on the floor of Congress. On October 17, 2003, voting against the Bush administration's request for another $87 billion with which to pursue its military adventures in Afghanistan and Iraq, Senator Robert Byrd (D.-W.Va.) met the occasion with the angry and plainspoken calling of a lie a lie:

---

election news was about something other than Al Gore's hairstyle or George Bush's English springer spaniel. Few of the people in the broadcast studios were old enough to remember ever having seen such a thing as democracy—the living organism as opposed to the old paintings and the marble statues—and to judge by the startled expressions in their faces, they didn't like the look of it. It hadn't been circumcised, and probably it was criminal. Congressman Connie Mack (R.-Fla.) shared the sentiment. Affronted by the spectacle of Democrats actually trying to win the election, he said, "They're politicizing the political process."

Taking the nation to war based on misleading rhetoric and hyped intelligence is a travesty and a tragedy. It is the most cynical of all cynical acts. It is dangerous to manipulate the truth. It is dangerous because once having lied, it is difficult to ever be believed again. Having misled the American people and stampeded them to war, this administration must attempt to sustain a policy predicated on falsehood. The president asks for billions from those same citizens who knew that they were misled about the need to go to war. We misinformed and insulted our friends and allies and now this administration is having more than a little trouble getting help from the international community. It is perilous to mislead. . . . I cannot support the politics of zeal and "might makes right" that created the new American arrogance in unilateralism that passes for foreign policy in this administration.

On November 9, 2003, in a speech delivered at Constitution Hall, two blocks west of the White House, Al Gore compounded the objection to the military spending with an objection to the administration's suppression of the freedoms of the American people:

The Bush administration's implicit assumption is that we have to sacrifice traditional freedoms in order to be safe from terrorists. This is simply untrue. It makes no more sense to launch an assault on civil liberties in order to get at terrorists, than it did to launch an invasion of Iraq to get Osama bin Laden.

In both cases the administration is attacking the wrong targets. In both cases, they have fostered false impressions, misled the nation and exploited public fears for partisan political gain. And in both cases they have used unprecedented secrecy to avoid accountability to Congress, the courts, the press and the people. . . .

The question before us could be of no greater moment. Will we continue to live as a people under the rule of law as embodied in our Constitution? Or will we fail future generations by leaving them a Constitution far diminished from the charter of liberty we have inherited from our forebears?

Answering Gore's questions in favor of the Constitution, two federal appeals courts (one in New York, the other in San Francisco) handed down rulings on December 18 against two of the Bush administration's seizures of executive power. The Second Circuit in New York decided that the president lacked the authority to detain indefinitely a United States citizen arrested on American soil on suspicion of terrorism simply by declaring him "an enemy combatant"; the Ninth Circuit in San Francisco declared that the administration's policy of imprisoning some 650 noncitizens captured in the Afghan war on a naval base at Guantánamo Bay, Cuba, without access to United States legal protections was unconstitutional as well as a violation of international law. Other voices in other rooms (among them those of Senator Bob Graham of Florida and former attorney general Ramsey Clark) put forward proposals for the impeachment of President Bush—

on grounds a good deal more substantial (betraying the Constitution, injuring the body politic) than the soiling of Monica Lewinsky's blue dress. The local authorities in more than a hundred American cities and towns passed resolutions urging the residents to resist the sweeping away of their civil liberties by federal agents who claim as pretext the prosecution of the war on terror. The language approved in Amherst, Massachusetts, can be taken as representative: "To the extent legally possible, no town employee shall officially assist or voluntarily cooperate in investigations, interrogations or arrest procedures that may be judged to violate civil rights or liberties." Equally representative was the objection voiced by Art Babbott, the city council member who sponsored the resolution in Flagstaff, Arizona. "We've been singing the same song in this country for more than 200 years," Babbott said. "It's a very good song and I want to keep singing it. I'm very leery of changing the lyrics."*

Babbott's uneasiness is well and truly placed. Every society can always count on the parties of reaction crying up the wish to make time stand still, seeking to hide from the storm of the world behind the walls of monumental bureaucracy

---

*City and county council resolutions opposing preemptive/unilateral war in Iraq passed in Arcata, Cotati, Culver City, and Oakland, California; Boulder, Crested Butte, and Denver, Colorado; Cornwall, New Haven, and Salisbury, Connecticut; Chicago and De Kalb, Illinois; Bar Harbor and Portland, Maine; Baltimore, Garrett Park, and Glen Echo, Maryland; Amherst, Boston, and Northampton, Massachusetts; Ann Arbor, Detroit, and Kalamazoo, Michigan; and so on. Cities that passed resolutions urging local noncooperation with federal authorities invading civil rights include Berkeley, Boulder, Cambridge, Chicago, and Santa Fe.

or within the choruses of adoring praise. Democratic self-government proceeds from a more courageous principle, allying itself with the proposition that the future is a work in progress and an act of imagination, not a pot of gold found somewhere over a Hollywood rainbow. At college in the 1950s I was taught to think of the twentieth century as the miraculous and happy ending to the story of human progress; I now think of the twenty-first century as a still-primitive beginning. From the perspective of the thirtieth century I expect the historians to look back on the works of our modern world as if on sand castles built by careless but sometimes surprisingly gifted children. Idealism rescues cynicism, and the presence of many individuals free to try the strength of their own imagination and intelligence assumes a ceaseless making and remaking, of laws and customs as well as of fortunes and matinee idols.

Among all the country's political virtues, candor is the one most necessary to the health and well-being of our mutual enterprise. Unless we try to tell one another the truth about what we know and think and see, we might as well amuse ourselves—for as long as somebody in uniform allows us to do so—with fairy tales. To the extent that a democratic society gives its citizens the chance to speak in their own voices and listens to what they have to say, it gives itself the chance not only of discovering its multiple glories and triumphs but also of surviving its multiple follies and crimes.

Index